THE
CURE

THE
CURE

THE DIVINE Rx
FOR THE BODY OF CHRIST—
LIFE-CHANGING LOVE

HARRY KRAUS, MD

CROSSWAY BOOKS

WHEATON, ILLINOIS

Cover photo: Veer
Cover design: Josh Dennis

First printing, 2008

Printed in the United States of America

ISBN 978-1-4335-0191-3
Mobipocket ISBN 978-1-4335-0420-4
PDF ISBN 1-978-1-4335-0419-8

Library of Congress Cataloging-in-Publication Data

Kraus, Harry Lee, 1960–
    The cure : the divine Rx for the body of Christ : life-changing love / Harry Kraus.
        p. cm.
    Includes bibliographical references and index.
    ISBN 978-1-4335-0191-3 (tpb : alk. paper)
        1. Love—Religious aspects—Christianity. 2. Body, Human—Religious aspects—Christianity. I. Title.
BV4639.K68 2008
241'.4—dc22
                                   2007049867

VP		16	15	14	13	12	11	10	09	08
		9	8	7	6	5	4	3	2	1

To my fellow Christians,
who though they have faltered along the way
have allowed the magnificence of God's grace
to inspire them to continue forward
as channels of the most powerful force in the universe
—love!

CONTENTS

8

ACKNOWLEDGMENTS

Special thanks to Ted Griffin for his input in the editing process. The manuscript is certainly stronger because of him. Thanks also to Noël Piper, who made valuable suggestions and helped me achieve the balance I needed.

INTRODUCTION

I'm tired. That's a bad thing. But that's a common thing for missionaries serving on foreign fields. In Africa, tiredness is almost a badge. I'm working hard for Jesus, you know. Others should notice and break into some sort of spontaneous expression of praise; if not directly to God, at least stop and pat me on the back. But this isn't a book about being exhausted for Christ, and in fact most of what I have to say will show you how futile and empty most of our precious work has become. Because we've strayed away from the main thing.

Yes, I'm tired. I am. But not like you might think. I'm tired of Christianity being misunderstood. Tired of Christianity being judged on the basis of Western culture. Tired of letting Hollywood define us, tired of materialism being the first love of the Christian, and tired of watching church growth being made up of disenchanted souls hopping from congregation to congregation instead of the lost swelling our ranks. I'm tired of seeing Islam make advances when I know the truth is on our side. Tired of seeing people embrace a religion that hides behind a cloak of lies while truth sits idle on the curb, ignored and forgotten.

We've strayed from the essence that defines us. We've left the main thing long behind, while we strive forward. We're busy. Fruitless. And don't forget that admirable missionary trait, tired.

We are awash with conferences and filled to the brim with discussions about methods for effective evangelism, contextualization, cell churches, culture-appropriate dress, and techniques for language acquisition. We talk about church planting strategies, partnership, and biblical visions for our eleventh-hour calling to complete the Great Commission. Just this week I attended a week-long missions conference where we spent more time learning about emergency contingency plans (in case an under-the-radar team in a creative access country is compromised), self-defense techniques, and spiritual warfare than we did about the main thing.

In fairness, the conference planners didn't really ignore the main thing. They just assumed the attendees (many were seasoned missionaries) had already mastered the main thing. So on we go with other items of importance while the very heartbeat of the gospel is sidelined.

Don't misunderstand. There are other important components of effective ministry. I am a huge proponent of thinking and acting strategically in planning outreach. An understanding of spiritual warfare is vital. There is even a place for study of safety issues and preventing possible hostile actions against missionaries who serve within environments unfriendly to Christians and our message. But it's still not the main thing.

I've spoken to dozens, perhaps hundreds of missionaries serving on foreign fields and many more Christians back home, and

I've concluded that most of us have tilted away from the core of God's motives behind the Great Commission. In a moment of profound tenderness we answered the call. But in the busyness of doing church, the heart of the gospel has faltered, its rhythm pathologic and in many cases expressing a fatal asystole. The heart of the gospel that once beat strong within is now stilled, registering a flat line, being ineffective and room-temperature dead.

Back home, the Christian church is facing its own onslaught of problems. The evils inherent to postmodernism, cultural irrelevance, the rising threat of Islam, and materialism need to be combated and overcome, but too many congregations are mired in pettiness, arguing over externals, worship styles, and schedules. The heartbeat of the gospel gasps beneath arguments over dress, programs, and budgets.

It's not like we deny the heart of the gospel. We give it mental assent, but in action we deemphasize its importance.

What am I talking about? *Agape.*

Love?

Yes, love. But I've called it by its Greek name to avoid the confusion and emotional baggage that swirls around this word that our culture has robbed of its meaning.

It's the most important component of effective evangelism. Remember what Paul tells us in 1 Corinthians 13?

> If I speak in the tongues of men and of angels, but have not love, I am a noisy gong or a clanging cymbal. And if I have prophetic powers, and understand all mysteries and all knowledge, and if I have all faith, so as to remove mountains, but have not love, I am nothing. If I give away all I have, and if I deliver up my body to be burned, but have not love, I gain nothing.
>
> —1 Corinthians 13:1–3

So there it is. The main thing. But that concept is so distorted by our contemporary culture that it's been left a dreamy emotion, a nebulous and fluffy feeling that we can't get our minds around and therefore ignore in our preparations for the work of the church. But without it we are nothing. All our strategies, partnerships, and efforts at contextualization, cell church, and programs are little more than an offbeat crashing of a cracked brass cymbal.

But I've never heard much more than a passing reference to love within the context of the mission of the church. "How-to" books abound. Want peace? Want to stop obsessing? Want to forgive? Want to be free from your past? Our libraries and bookstores will be glad you've stopped in. Hundreds of titles will assist in your search.

But I need to love my neighbor. I need to love my brothers and sisters in Christ. And leave it to Jesus to make my life even more difficult when he said, "Love your enemies."

Jesus didn't make it optional. Over and over the injunction to love is issued in the strongest language.

> "A new commandment I give to you, that you love one another: just as I have loved you, you also are to love one another."
>
> —John 13:34

> "This is my commandment, that you love one another as I have loved you."
>
> —John 15:12

But I can't just respond to a command and love, can I? Jesus can't be serious.

Or is he?

Why do we ignore love? Perhaps we just assume the basics are, well, just that—basic. Been there. Done that. Of course, there's love. Every Christian knows that God is love. We all sang it loudly in Sunday school. And all of us memorized John 3:16. Some of us even mastered 1 Corinthians 13, the *love* chapter. So where is it? Does it really define us as we were told it would? Is it possible that the church has just moved on to other, less ethereal topics and left love for those who are honeymooning with their faith? Has love been relegated to a syrupy-sweet, dreamy emotion, unworthy of serious time and study? Is there really anything syrupy-sweet about dying in agony on a jagged, bloodstained cross?

Maybe we've been looking at it all wrong. But we can't afford to do that. Having a correct theology of *agape*—God's love for us, especially seen in his Son's death in our place, now flowing through us to others—beats at the very heart of the gospel.

To uncover the answers, we need to back up from the love chapter of 1 Corinthians 13 to examine the metaphor Paul uses to describe the church in 1 Corinthians 12. We, the church, are *the body of Christ.* I've spent most of my adult life preparing for and practicing the art of surgery, performing thousands of dissections in an attempt to change the effects of pathology (illness). My prayer is that within these pages, through a careful dissection of Paul's metaphor, we'll come to an understanding together about Christ's command (love!) and how to fulfill it.

So let's begin.

Down with clanging cymbals. Up with the basic mission of the church. It starts within the heart of every believer.

Love!

For Further Reflection

1. "We've strayed from the essence that defines us. We've left the main thing long behind, while we strive forward." Do you agree or disagree? Why?

2. What is *agape* love? What is its source, and where do we see it most clearly? How is it different from the love we normally practice or seek?

3. Why are there so many "how-to" Christian books but so few books on the importance of love in and through the church?

4. What did Jesus say should be the telltale sign that we are his people? What is the key verse for his command on this? How are you, or your church, doing in this area?

5. What is the heart of the gospel, its driving force or central truth? What does this mean to you personally?

Part One

His Mandate—
Our Mission—Love

Chapter One

THE GREATEST COMMISSION

A s I begin this chapter, I'm writing in one of those places I call a Christian-theology-meets-the-road kind of place. It's a place of scorching heat and sand, a place I can't believe anyone calls a refuge, but that's exactly what it's called by 160,000 Somali refugees.

Dadaab, Kenya, is the home of three, soon to be four UN refugee camps just inside the Kenya border next to Somalia. For many, it's home to a life robbed of hope, a barely-make-it existence made tolerable because of free food rations and the absence of active war. Which, by the way, is why it's a refuge. The problem with the camps here is that a temporary situation has turned agonizingly permanent for so many. Resettlement, the mantra of the United Nations High Commission for Refugees, has been next to impossible for the Somali people because of what seems to be nearly ceaseless government instability and anarchy. So, for thousands a few months has turned into fifteen years. And time in Dadaab crawls with a determined and sweaty sluggishness.

For me, at this moment, life is good. My face is sixteen inches from a fan set on the highest speed. I finished my day of surgery in the primitive camp hospital, took a lukewarm shower (not that I have any choice about the temperature, mind you; it just comes straight out of the single tap that way), and now have only another hour before the sun will dive straight into the equatorial horizon and relieve everyone else who isn't so blessed to be sitting in front of an electric fan.

In a casual moment I might even tell you, "I love my fan," and that would be true, but it only illustrates something else that bugs me about common English language. We use the word *love* with such cavalier abandon that when we stop to think about it in the context of proper theology, it takes us a while to understand that its biblical meaning is huge in comparison.

I can't be here without remembering my first visit. I was helping run a surgery clinic and was short on time late one afternoon. My translators kept telling me, "You have to leave. The driver is here. The other passengers are waiting."

I looked around and realized there would be no satisfaction for the dozens of patients who remained. Try and imagine what it was like. The closest thing I can say to paint an accurate picture in your mind is that it's like seeing patients in an old outbuilding you'd see in the Midwest, one of those drafty barns with a corrugated metal roof, a cement floor, and unfinished boards lining the walls, luckily with cracks between the boards so they let a little extra light in along with a welcome breeze. There were a few wooden chairs, a desk, and a hard table where patients could lie down for an exam. I think the patients knew I had to leave. In the last ten minutes, half of the patients waiting outside squeezed in around us, each one pushing a ragged collection of papers in his or her fists toward my face. It was the camp's way of doing medical records. The patients keep all of the handwritten notes from all of their visits, each one folded and refolded until they are torn along the seams. How to unfold them was the puzzle at the beginning of each patient visit.

"Dhaktar! You need to go."

I held up my hands. I was missionary-tired and didn't want to be the bad guy to send everyone away. If I surrendered, at least I hoped the patients would see I was being forced to close the clinic for the day.

My eyes fell upon a woman sitting at the corner of my desk. She'd insinuated herself into position and had sat quietly while I'd been interviewing and examining the previous patient. Medical privacy, I've discovered, is a relative concept. A necessary and valued concept in the West, but in the refugee camps, giving the patient ahead of you privacy might mean you'll never be seen because many others will crowd in ahead of you.

I sighed. The woman had been waiting so patiently. I couldn't just leave her. "What about her?" I said.

Now my assistant sighed. "Okay. But this is the last one."

With the clock ticking and my driver waiting in the heat with all the other passengers, I waited impatiently for the answers to my questions. "Why is she here?"

The woman sat in silence.

I repeated my question.

She leaned closer to my translator. He looked at me. "She won't say unless she's in private."

I looked around. *Privacy here?* Dozens of patients and a few staff members had crowded into the two-room building. In the corner of the room, a wooden table was partially hidden by a portable fabric screen. It would have to do.

I retreated with my patient and a translator. Once in the corner, the woman began to talk.

Now, I need you to understand that she was dressed like a typical Somali woman. Somali people are all Muslims. Okay, not all, but 99.9 percent, and this woman was clothed modestly like most of them. I could see the front of her face only. Her neck, cheeks, and the top of her head were veiled. As I studied her face, I got a gut-check discomfort. My patient was just too masculine to be dressed the way she was.

After some discussion, which seemed intolerably long because the car was waiting, the translator turned to me with a matter-of-fact tone. "She wants you to tell her whether she's a man or a woman."

Immediately I understood that I wouldn't be able to answer her question while the driver was waiting. I asked her to lie down and made sure the portable screen offered a for-our-eyes-only exam for myself and my medical translator.

I began my exam with the genitalia and immediately understood the confusion. I was confused at first too. I had suspicions that the patient suffered from a combination of common anomalies that were both easily correctable. The crime of it was that because she'd been raised in the bush with little access to medical care, her parents made an assumption based on a best guess. And so my patient had spent the first thirty-five years of her life as a female.

My heart was touched. Only where medical care is unavailable, only where despair and fatalism rule can such a tragedy unfold. *Africa.* "I'm not sure," I said. "But we'll bring you to Kijabe Hospital. A few easy tests will tell us the answer."

Why tell that story now? Because as we begin exploring the great metaphor that likens the church to the body of Christ, I wanted to go back to the very basic thing that defines us all, the very wonderful and marvelous molecule known as our DNA.

You see, from the very moment of conception each of us inherits DNA from our parents. DNA is a helical-shaped molecule with two strands. Think of a ladder that's been twisted so that the normally parallel uprights curl around each other. We got one strand from dad, the other from mom.

Our DNA contains the genetic code, some thirty thousand genes that are code for all the amazing proteins that make up the structure and guide the chemical processes of our life. It's all quite incredible and a bit mystifying, but suffice it to say that within our DNA are the basic blueprints that define everything about us. Everything! Blue eyes. Curly hair. When we're going to have a growth spurt and how tall we'll grow as a result (assuming we have the proper nourishment). Less well understood, but equally important are features such as a tendency toward depression, colon cancer, and a propensity to alcohol dependency.

So, for my patient in the refugee camp this was all true. A message resided in every nucleated cell revealing the identity as male or female. As far as determination of sex is concerned, we all learned in high-school biology that XX equals female and XY equals male. The problem with my patient wasn't that the cells didn't have the message. The message had just been scrambled a bit in development.

A DNA fingerprint is the unique feature that has turned forensic evidence for or against thousands of people suspected of committing crimes. A woman is attacked, defending herself by scratching her assailant. Later skin cells are collected from beneath her fingernails. The DNA from those cells is examined, revealing a perfect blueprint unique to the perpetrator, assuming the criminal isn't an identical twin.

DNA present within the cells provides an exact identification. What about the body of Christ? Is there a feature that can provide the proof that will convict us of belonging to Jesus? Is there enough forensic evidence left in our wake to identify us as individual members of his body?

Has a vital message been scrambled?

Take time this week and ask the people around you if there is any observable feature that sets a person apart and lets you know that he or she is a Christian. The answers you hear may be encouraging. Or a bit threatening.

Speaking from the viewpoint of a missionary, having lived around people of several different worldviews, I'll encourage you to be sure that your answer has nothing to do with Western culture. In short, it can have nothing to do with externals. It has to be something within us that, given appropriate nourishment, will result in a defining quality.

Jesus gives us the answer.

> "By this all people will know that you are my disciples, if you have love for one another."
>
> —John 13:35

After ten of the original twelve apostles were martyred for their faith in Christ, John lived on, the only apostle to live into old age. And in those years, the message he heard from Jesus resonated and matured within him and was revived by the Holy Spirit in the following passage:

> Little children, let us not love in word or talk but in
> deed and in truth. By this we shall know that we are
> of the truth and reassure our heart before him.
>
> —1 John 3:18–19

And again, a little later,

> Beloved, let us love one another, for love is from
> God, and whoever loves has been born of God and
> knows God.
>
> —1 John 4:7

Can we ask for a clearer answer than this?

Unfortunately, around the world, particularly in areas of Muslim dominance, Christianity is confused with Western culture and has nothing to do with love. In the age of the Internet and videos, Christians are defined by the dress of Hollywood's elite. To the missionary's dismay, Christianity is defined by American culture and American politics. It's an unfair assumption, but one we have to deal with nonetheless. "Christian America" defines my faith in the minds of anyone not willing to take a critical look at Jesus.

I made a trip last month into Somaliland to teach in a struggling medical school. During my stay, U.S. jets bombed suspected terrorist sites in Mogadishu, the capital city of Somalia to the south. While Somaliland considers itself independent from Somalia, there is nothing like an attack involving U.S. forces to raise concern for their southern neighbors.

"Mr. Bush is a Christian," one Somalilander said to me. "Why does he behave in this way?"

I wanted to steer clear of political topics. If I defended President Bush, I would have precipitated more difficult questions. But to condemn the President would have been a denial of my own conscience. My country had just attacked theirs. It hardly seemed wise to praise my government's decision from within their borders, *even though I thought the attack was justified.* I responded, "It's best to judge Christianity from a close examination of Jesus Christ, not from the actions of Christians."

Was my answer a cop-out? Perhaps, but I know there are many times when I don't want Christianity defined by my life.

I think criticism of Christianity on the basis of Christians is bogus, but unfortunately our actions can become stumbling blocks for others who are considering the faith. I've spoken to Muslims who are offended by people judging Islam on the basis of suicide bombers, so I guess I understand the predicament.

"By this all people will know . . ." These words can be hammer-blows to our consciences. I wince at the memory of numerous times I've acted in ways that were nothing like love. But these words are not meant to discourage. John certainly knew that we would be unloving. Hadn't he just said, in chapter 2 of 1 John (see especially verses 1–2), that our sins have been forgiven?

The truth remains: love is to be the defining, dominant characteristic of the body of Christ, the evidence of our discipleship to a world longing for love.

The rub is in the "how to." I'll get to that later. Suffice it to say that so much of the process begins with an understanding of our need.

Love isn't an optional fruit. I believe in the indwelling of God's Spirit, though it's a bit hard to get my mind around that fact. Nonetheless, I believe in "Christ in me." Paul refers to this as a mystery, so I don't feel too cranially challenged for not getting it myself.

> To them God chose to make known how great among
> the Gentiles are the riches of the glory of this mystery,
> which is Christ in you, the hope of glory.
>
> —Colossians 1:27

If God resides in me and he defines himself as love, then I have to believe that love has taken up residence in me in some way. His character may not be completely manifest in me, but I believe that must be my fault, not his.

Let's go back to our analogy. The DNA sends a definite message to every nucleated cell: "Be male" or "be female." The message will be translated and retranslated, but the end result is structural proteins that make a person either male or female. In the case of my patient at the refugee camp, the message was clear at its origin (the DNA), but it became a bit mixed during the last few steps, resulting in a male without all of the externals being completely developed. We made this diagnosis by doing a simple biopsy. The hard part was determining what to do next. Suffice it to say, I had a long conversation with my patient! Often in these cases a clear gender identification has occurred because of the way the person has been raised. Not so in the case of my patient, who had always felt male and wanted to be male. Fortunately the man had a few relatively simple anomalies that combined to lead to his parents' (and his) confusion. Each defect was corrected surgically, and he returned to a different refugee camp as a male.

Likewise, a clear message has gone out to every member of Christ's body: "Love!" Over and over, like the DNA message sent to every cell, the message is unmistakable. Love! Jesus issues it as an order, calling it "a new commandment" (John 13:34) or "my commandment" (John 15:12). That's strong language. It's not a suggestion but a clear mandate. In fact, the language could not be more forceful and is certainly as powerful (and more frequent) as the instructions we know as the Great Commission. I believe if we as the body of Christ would focus as much attention on loving each other and loving our neighbors (and the rest of a love-starved world), we might just find the Great Commission occurring as naturally as smoke follows fire. Hand in hand. And maybe that was Jesus' point, after all.

Lots of things can happen to scramble a DNA message, to hamper its full instigation in every cell. Competing messages, inadequate nutrition, or illness can interfere with a cell's ability to respond. *But the DNA reveals the way things were intended to be.*

Some of you are uncomfortable with my analogy. We're uneasy hearing such stories of gender confusion. And yet I have the audacity to use it in a spiritual analogy. Why? Because a condition like my patient's is a tragedy; just hearing about it makes us ill at ease. Don't get me wrong! It's appropriate to recoil at such an example, but I really want you to see the parallel tragedy that is occurring every day in the body of Christ.

My patient's life was a heartbreaking misfortune, a real tragedy. He lived for thirty-five years not understanding who he was. Because of access to medical care, calamities like this are avoided in the developed world. But not in the Horn of Africa. We look on with a sense of shock and revulsion. *This all could have been avoided!*

But where is our shock over the defining condition of the body of Christ? God's clear message of love has been scrambled. We are carrying the DNA message that defines us, but we are confused about our identity. The world looks on, and they don't know either. Is the Christian church known for love? Or something less holy? This is the true tragedy that should make us recoil in disgust.

I cringe to hear how Christianity is thought of within some Muslim circles. We're misunderstood, and our teachings are twisted. We're known for the escapades of our Hollywood celebrities, agents who unwillingly stand for Christianity because they come from a "Christian" nation. Confusion like this is understood when you realize that there is no separation of church and state within the religion of Islam.

What is more disturbing is when I find myself recoiling from the truth of accusations that Christ's church stands for malice, ill will, and intolerance. Listen to the sometimes too-true words of Spinoza, a Jewish philosopher:

> I have often wondered that persons who make boast of professing the Christian religion—namely love, joy, peace, temperance, and charity to all men—should quarrel with such rancorous animosity and display daily towards one another such bitter hatred, that this, rather than the virtues they profess, is the readiest criteria of their faith.

The problem lies within all of us. We're more conscious of our sin than of God's love. We've feasted on judgment and justice instead of grace. We've given mental assent to the truth that God loves us, but little more. Our souls remain crusty, with our receivers tuned only to our own negative runaway thoughts. Or worse, we've tuned our ears to the deceiver himself. *You're unlovely.*

But the solution lies within each member of the body of Christ. *What? Didn't you just say the* problem *lies within us? And now you say the* answer *is there too?*

You see, accepting God's love message accelerates a transformation of the heart.

When Christ, love personified, entered my heart, he sent out a message of love, a message of *the way things were intended to be.*

What are the things that keep me from responding? Has Christ's command been scrambled along the way?

Sometimes, for me, the answer is yes. Not always, mind you. And the good news is, there is a remedy for the times when my heart can't seem to find a way to love. Can you bear to have me continue my analogy? Spiritual remedies may require a spiritual scalpel of sorts. This is sometimes painful, but very often this is just what the doctor ordered.

We'll talk about that a bit later.

For Further Reflection

1. Do you agree that the body of Christ, the church, has a DNA? How would you define or describe that DNA?

2. In what ways do people confuse true Christianity with Western or American culture? How would you help individuals see the difference?

3. Do you agree that "Love isn't an optional fruit"? How visible is this fruit in your life? What actions do you need to take to allow it to blossom more in you?

4. Do you agree that "if we as the body of Christ would focus as much attention on loving each other and loving our neighbors (and the rest of a love-starved world), we might just find the Great Commission occurring as naturally as smoke follows fire"? Why or why not?

5. Is the Christian church generally known for love for God and one another or for something else? If the latter, what? Were Spinoza's caustic remarks too harsh or on-target?

Chapter Two

THE LOVE-SHAPED VOID

I remember my first love note. I was in fifth grade. Her name was Jodi, she had short blonde hair, and she claimed to be a distant cousin of Paul McCartney of the Beatles. That last fact was enough to make her dangerously alluring in my mind. I was brought up in the Mennonite church, you see, and I saw everything in terms of two boxes: church and worldly. The second box was a lot bigger than the first.

Here's how it worked for me. I knew Mennonites were heaven-bound. I knew there were other Christians out there, but beyond my congregation everything and everybody was suspect. We were pretty big on being separate. Putting some things in the boxes was easy. The radio was definitely worldly. In fact, pretty much all music was worldly, unless it was a cappella like our singing on Sunday mornings. My mother's starting to cart me downtown to take violin lessons muddied my think-

ing about music instruments being worldly. I figured since she
seemed to think it was okay, I'd start unloading some music
from the worldly box, but only classical initially. God liked
classical music. The fact that my classical violin teacher smoked
cigarettes and my mom still liked him was troubling. Smoking
was definitely worldly, and we were supposed to be separate.
Also anyone who worshiped in a church where the American
flag was displayed was seriously in question. And when I started
public school in the fifth grade (having attended a Mennonite
school for the first four years), I felt guilty saying the Pledge of
Allegiance. But that's where I met Jodi, the cute blonde, and
my heart first felt the stirrings of alluring conflict.

Not that Jodi was the first woman in my life. I'd even held
hands with a girl before, once when I was in fourth grade, but
that was with a safe Mennonite girl named Rachel.

Pop music, especially sung by guys who needed haircuts, was
completely off-limits. The Beatles were definitely in the worldly
box. Oh well, Paul McCartney was just supposed to be a distant
cousin anyway, so maybe Jodi wasn't *that* worldly.

The day she handed me a small folded note, I could hardly
wait to get into a private place to read it. And not just read
it. Memorize it. Every word. And everything in between the
words, poring over each short line to squeeze out the emotions
behind it. She said she loved me!

And, oh yeah, she wrote at the end, "Don't tell Kevin."

Kevin was one of my friends. Later we were on the junior
high wrestling team together. I think she wrote Kevin the same
note and said, "Don't tell Harry."

I didn't figure that out until later. Much later.

I took the letter home and hid it in the battery compartment
of an old transistor radio. It wasn't really mine, just one my
parents had stopped using and I inherited. I had inherited their

old bed, too. It was a double bed with a built-in cabinet for a headboard. That's where I kept the radio. It couldn't play a tune without the batteries, but to me, the music hidden inside was pure heaven. Love. The cute blonde said she loved me.

My bedroom was downstairs in the basement. Everyone else in the family lived upstairs. My parents said it would be fun for the guy of the house (other than my dad, and I knew he wasn't moving down there) to have some independence. Later I realized I'd moved downstairs where my mother wouldn't have to listen to my violin.

I'd lie in my bed at night and slide off the cover to the battery compartment of the radio. I'd unfold the note as if it would break if I handled it too carelessly. Then I'd stare at the words by flashlight. I didn't need to read them. I knew every word.

Why did my heart thrill at knowing someone cared enough for me to use the *l* word?

Because I'm wired the way you are. In fact, I believe we're all wired that way. We all want to be loved.

What Blaise Pascal, the seventeenth-century philosopher, said about there being a "God-shaped void" in every human heart seems a little suspect to me. Okay, I know what his point was, and everyone may have a void that only God can fill, though they don't really know what they want. But truer than that is what I call a love-shaped void. The human heart is just made that way. And we know it. There's no mystery about what we want. Everyone wants to be loved.

In the last chapter I told you that we're wired to *give* love. It's at the core of who we've been created to be, in our spiritual DNA, so to speak. Now I want to shift focus a bit and look at the other side: we've been created to *receive* love, and the reason for that stands at the center of a right theology: God loves me. And you.

But perhaps we've grown complacent about this, in the same way that so many respond to the old children's song. "Jesus loves me! This I know." It's old. Simplistic. But it beats at the heart of the gospel.

I wanted to talk about this at the beginning, because this is where it all starts. A correct understanding about biblical love begins in the heart of God. He defines love—"God is love" (1 John 4:8).

> In this is love, not that we have loved God but that he loved us and sent his Son to be the propitiation for our sins.
>
> —1 John 4:10

> God shows his love for us in that while we were still sinners, Christ died for us.
>
> —Romans 5:8

> But God, being rich in mercy, because of the great love with which he loved us, even when we were dead in our trespasses, made us alive together with Christ—by grace you have been saved.
>
> —Ephesians 2:4–5

> By this we know love, that he laid down his life for us.
>
> —1 John 3:16a

Want a correct theology of love? This is where it begins. Not that we love God, but that he loves us.

This knowledge is the start of being able to send the message of love into the world around us. It should go without saying (but I'll say it anyway) that this message is better walked than talked. Words are important, but love, as we'll see in subsequent chapters, is a real get-your-hands-dirty sort of concept.

All Christians will tell you they believe this. "Yeah, I know, God loves me." But for most, the words tumble from their lips, but their souls remain sluggish, barely registering a blip on the emotional radar screen. I'm puzzled about this indifference in the presence of such amazing love.

It's true. We've been desensitized to the presence of the Almighty. Just as a recurrent nerve stimulus results in a lesser and lesser response, our souls seem to have enfolded themselves in a casual blanket, so that we are shielded from reacting. We ho-hum ourselves through Sunday morning worship, blind to the brightness of God's glory, cavalier to the awesomeness of the fact that *God loves me!*

Remember the precautions that the high priest took before entering the presence of God in the Holy of Holies? According to legend (not the Bible), a rope was tied around his ankle, so he could be retrieved in case something went wrong and he needed to be pulled out from the awesome and terrible presence of God. What if we posted two burly men at the entrance to our next church gathering? Sleeves rolled up to reveal their bulging biceps, they would carefully attach a rope to each worshiper who approached. "Careful, brother," the attendant cautions as he ties the rope to your ankle. "You are entering the presence of the Almighty, the King of kings, the Lord of lords, the Creator of the universe. Be blessed."

The knot is secured and tested, and you feel your stomach tighten as you realize the gravity of the moment. Your eyes meet those of the attendant. His expression is sober, his eyes grave.

How would we proceed? With such a reminder, would we dare enter with the yawning attitude that is endemic in our gatherings?

God loves us. This is an explosive, life-altering message. But how human to not believe it, or to allow our thoughts to cascade into a thousand other self-demeaning directions. How dare we call unlovely what he has loved with the price of the cross! Yes, God loves us—unconditionally, totally, genuinely. But his love is not a wispy or wimpy "Because I love you I will never hassle you about your behavior or call you to account for the ways you disobeyed me." His love demands that we admit our sinfulness, and yet also makes a way of forgiveness—the death of Jesus in our place. Sadly, we pay too little attention to this great love.

But neither our flat denial nor our complacency toward his love can be our focus just yet. Later we will look in some detail at the pathologies that lie at the root of our failure to find his love to be the incredible and mind-blowing reality that it is.

For now let us look more closely at this mountaintop concept—that God loves his children, his bride, and nothing can stand in love's way.

> Who shall separate us from the love of Christ? Shall tribulation, or distress, or persecution, or famine, or nakedness, or danger, or sword? . . . No, in all these things we are more than conquerors through him who loved us. For I am sure that neither death nor life, nor angels nor rulers, nor things present nor things to come, nor powers, nor height nor depth, nor anything else in all creation, will be able to separate us from the love of God in Christ Jesus our Lord.
>
> —Romans 8:35–39

What incredible news! Nothing can separate us from God's love. Not even my particular temperament or my feelings. Nothing. Period.

This news should be the source of a never-ending refreshing, a spring so cool that it never ceases to satisfy. This news should prompt an overflow of love into the world around us and form the basis for the message we share to initiate the formation of new disciples—in effect, a fulfillment of the Great Commission.

Not sharing this love is antithetical to its very nature. Our mission as Christians is made easy when we are dwelling in the reality of Romans 8. God's love motivated a daring plan for our rescue. It was a mission straight from his heart, but it did not begin with Jesus' oft-quoted words in Matthew 28. Missions finds its beginning within the paradise of a garden:[1]

> And they heard the sound of the LORD God walking in the garden in the cool of the day, and the man and his wife hid themselves from the presence of the LORD God among the trees of the garden. But the LORD God called to the man and said to him, "Where are you?"
>
> —Genesis 3:8–9

That's the beginning of mission—God searching for his beloved, a search that would require the substitutionary death of his own Son. And the love that motivated his search spurs us forward in an attempt to bring the gospel to every tongue, tribe, and nation.

I love the way Eugene Peterson says it in his popular paraphrase:

> Long before he laid down earth's foundations, he had
> us in mind, had settled on us as the focus of his love,
> to be made whole and holy by his love. . . . (What
> pleasure he took in planning this!) He wanted us to
> enter into the celebration of his lavish gift-giving by
> the hand of his beloved Son.
>
> —Ephesians 1:4–7, *Message*

Our own culture suffers for lack of a word strong enough to understand the depth or strength of God's feelings toward us. We use the word *love* so casually. I love my laptop. I love the Atlanta Braves. You know what I mean. So we get our ideas of what God's love is like in small glimpses.

A few days ago I saw a little boy, a toddler who could just begin to pronounce "Daddy." It came out more like "Da-ye." He'd been separated from his father for a few hours during a conference meeting. When he saw his father a few feet away, he began to call out to his dad. He was uninhibited. Joyous. With arms lifted in anticipation as he ran forward. "Da-ye! Da-ye! Da-ye!"

I looked up to see his father's delight. Eyes bright. A smile on his face. His arms open to scoop his little son into his arms.

Think of the tenderness shown as a parent covers a sleeping child in the nursery. Think of a nurse bathing and dressing a patient too weak to care for himself. Picture joyous airport reunions between lovers. Tender words shared between husband and wife. A gentle caress, a kiss, an intimate moment. Cool water given to a stranger. Going the second mile, beyond any expectation.

Pull these images around you, and find your own examples to provide just a shadow of God's love for us.

What examples can we pull from Holy Scripture? Here's one of my favorite images, that of our Heavenly Father rejoicing over his bride:

> The LORD your God is in your midst, a mighty one who will save; he will rejoice over you with gladness; he will quiet you by his love; he will exult over you with loud singing.
>
> —Zephaniah 3:17

Other examples abound. The father of the prodigal son running forward to greet him. Jesus touching, healing, feeding, and encouraging. The entire book of Song of Solomon.

All of these and even the picture of love between bride and bridegroom fall short of giving us an adequate idea of the greatness of God's love for us.

> For as high as the heavens are above the earth, so great is his steadfast love toward those who fear him.
>
> —Psalm 103:11

And do I need to remind you that because of grace, his love is given freely and without condition? The twin truths that there is nothing I can do to make him love me more and nothing I can do to make him love me less are liberating in their effect on the soul who truly embraces them. Not that his love for and delight in us should be our greatest preoccupation—bringing glory to and delighting in him should be our highest desire and goal. Nevertheless, we do delight in his love for us, for without it we would be hopelessly condemned and lost.

We cannot delve far into a study of *agape* without looking at 1 Corinthians 13.

> Love is patient and kind; love does not envy or boast;
> it is not arrogant or rude. It does not insist on its
> own way; it is not irritable or resentful; it does not
> rejoice at wrongdoing, but rejoices with the truth.
> Love bears all things, believes all things, hopes all
> things, endures all things.
>
> —1 Corinthians 13:4–7

Here Paul holds up the standard of love, defining it, revealing how it should look in expression by the body of Christ. But in order to express it fully, we need to come to grips with the fact that first God loves me.

The effect of the simple yet profound truth that God loves me is huge. Within the confidence of his love, there is no need for worry. I no longer need to impress anyone. There is no need for despair over my circumstances. If I am sure that God loves me, I am confident he will work and keep working on my behalf. I can pray with assurance, preach with confidence, smile with sincerity, obey without concern for my own welfare, follow faithfully in the presence of trial or darkness, and share generously. When I know God's love, I can be strong against temptation, stand unmoving in the midst of persecution, and remain unafraid in the presence of danger. When I understand love, I'm free from the bondage of the past, the anxiety of the present, and fear of the future.

If you understand God's love for you, *really understand it*, you will change the world.

Knowing divine love's sacrifice enables me to sacrifice. My time, my need for convenience, and my comfort are all on the altar. The soul that is confident in the Father's love is a soul at rest, a soul who needs not be concerned with the opinions of others and is free to enjoy creation as it was intended, a gift for our pleasure. The believer who is secure in God's love is a powerful force, an effective witness, and an encouragement to fellow Christians. So what if illness, poverty, or unwanted circumstances come our way? They cannot defeat the soul whose anchor is the love of God.

Understanding God's passion for us opens the way for him to be our first love, our greatest passion, and the source of our satisfaction. Without understanding this, we will fill our love-shaped voids with substitutes that can never satisfy like Jesus can.

Oh, how I hope that you will not only give this truth a mental nod but will embrace it with your whole heart. Meditate on the promises of his love until your soul is alive, invigorated, and swept away in the joy of being God's beloved. Make it your aim to have your identity first and foremost wrapped up in this, that you are his delight, that you are the object of his passion, and that forever you will be his beloved. But again, let's not make this into a selfish preoccupation. Yes, God loves us with all his being, and that is our delight. But it is also true, as John Piper has expressed it, that "The love of God is not God's making much of us, but God's saving us from self-centeredness so that we can enjoy making much of him forever."[2]

Everything that follows grows not from our loving him or loving others but from his loving us.

When I was in the fifth grade, I needed only to steal away for a few minutes alone in my room and read Jodi's note to quicken my pulse and feel afresh the thrill of being loved.

Today I can steal away again and read another love letter of sorts, personalizing it and hiding it away in my heart. "Long before I laid down earth's foundations, I had you in mind, had settled on you as the focus of my love" (Ephesians 1:4, *Message*, pronoun changes mine).

And I can just imagine the ending: "Share this with Kevin."

For Further Reflection

1. Do you agree that there is a God-shaped void, a love-shaped void, in every human heart? Why is this so? What does this really mean?

2. What does Scripture mean when it says that "God is love"? What does this mean for you personally?

3. Do you think you have become desensitized to the presence of God? How do you respond to reminders that God loves you—with doubt, worship, ho-hum, or denial?

4. Do you agree that you can do nothing to make God love you more and nothing to make God love you less? Why or why not?

5. How can understanding, really grasping and leaning on, the reality of God's love for you benefit you emotionally, spiritually, in your relationships, and in other ways?

Chapter Three

A CONTROLLING PASSION

I've had my share of disaster dates. As a senior in high school, I attended a boarding school four hours west of my home in Tidewater, Virginia. Eastern Mennonite High School was far enough away from my parents to give me a taste of college dorm life and give me a little independence, something I didn't always use in the best way. Dating without direct parental supervision can be exhilarating. Or humiliating. I remember one date that started so badly, I don't remember anything beyond the first five minutes.

She was a pretty girl. She had dark hair and blue eyes, a fairly rare genetic combination, really. Striking. This girl was a farm girl. Not a priss. A girl you could take on a hike and she wouldn't be afraid she'd break a nail. She was the kind of girl I could think about for five minutes straight, something to oc-

cupy my mind between snacks or whatever else consumed my
mind as a seventeen-year-old male. And that was the source of
the problem. Sometimes I had my mind on the girl more than
on important basics.

I was using my dad's pale yellow Subaru two-door sedan
with a four-speed manual transmission. Manual transmissions
impress girls, even if you're driving an old sedan. I drove out
to the farm where she lived, parked the car, went to the door
of the old white farmhouse, and knocked on the front door.
She was waiting for me there. She was expecting me. I wasn't
disappointed. She smiled at me, her blue eyes sparkling. We
started walking out toward the lane.

But something was wrong. Seriously wrong. My father's
Subaru, the pale yellow one with the manual transmission,
destined to help me impress my date, had vanished. I'd only
been away from the car for a few moments. My mind began to
race. *Where's the car? Is this some sort of a cruel joke by some
of my buddies?* My next thoughts were that this was a sinister
act. *A crime? Thievery?* I shook my head. This wasn't the big
city; it was rural Virginia.

The blue-eyed girl broke my tortured silence. "What'd you
park down there for?"

I was dumbfounded. "Down where?"

She pointed down the hill. A hill. I hadn't even noticed there
was a bit of a hill. Duh.

Some of you are beginning to understand. I hadn't set the
parking brake, *and* I'd left the car in neutral. On manual transmission cars, that's a big mistake.

The car had made an amazing journey without me. Down
the hill and over a cattle guard, one of those metal-barred con-
traptions set in the ground that cows can't walk over. Through

an open gate without scraping either side of the fence opening. Coasting forward, picking up speed, racing down the hill.

It gets worse. Picture the layout of the land, something I hadn't paid attention to because my mind was on the girl. A pond sat on one side, a barn-like shed straight ahead. And the car raced forward with no one controlling it. If a problem with a moving vehicle ends in disaster, it's probably due to a lack of a higher power controlling the vehicle.

And in life (you knew there was a point to all of this), without control we are like a runaway car headed for disaster. In his second letter to the Corinthians, Paul slips a phrase into a discussion about our ministry to others. It is easy to pass over, but it highlights the key to understanding Paul and his motivation to sacrifice and serve.

> For the love of Christ controls us. . . .
> —2 Corinthians 5:14a

It's true that what you love controls you, determines what you think about, affects your choices, and establishes your path on life's highway. When asked by a lawyer what is needed to inherit eternal life, Jesus' answer was straightforward.

> "You shall love the Lord your God with all your heart and with all your soul and with all your strength and with all your mind, and your neighbor as yourself."
> —Luke 10:27

On another occasion when asked what the greatest commandment is, Jesus' answer was the same. Love God. And not just a little. Worship him—with all your heart, soul, mind, and strength.

I believe that loving God is the natural response to having his love poured into our hearts. In the last chapter I said, "If you understand God's love for you, *really understand it*, you will change the world." I believe that. But the first thing that happens as a natural response to understanding that God loves you is that you love him back. This is the essence of heartfelt worship. We've made a few steps into this journey, but we'll never travel far from the huge truth that God loves us, as evidenced in so many ways, but particularly in his Son's paying for our sins on the cross. Everything else, especially finding our way to love God and our neighbors, flows out as a result of soaking in that truth.

Three Problems

In Jesus' answer, he holds up the twin towers of our faith. The Christian life is to be all about loving God and loving our neighbor. Since these are held up over and over as the standard, we should take notice and concentrate on them. Yet somehow it seems that love has been shifted to the periphery of Christian thought. Love is thought of as a suitable devotional topic, but little more. Ask anyone on the street how to tell if someone is a Christian. The answers might surprise you and will likely include defining us by *what we don't do*. Christians don't smoke. Christians don't dance. Okay, maybe in today's world they wouldn't say that one, but maybe they'd say Christians don't dance well. What would surprise me is if they said, "You can tell because of their love for one another." How has love been sidelined from the center of Christian practice and theology?

Loving God is to be our first and highest call. Shouldn't loving him flow naturally from the absolutely amazing news that he is passionate about us, his bride?

It should. But perhaps that's part of the problem. We see it in terms of a "should have" instead of a "get to."

Why isn't the love of God the controlling passion of our lives? The answer has three parts, three possibilities. First, we don't know God. Second, we don't believe what we know. Third, someone or something has taken God's place.

Let's consider these one at a time. I am to love God with all my heart, soul, mind, and strength. Yet sadly, there are times when I'm not "in love" with him. The first reason may be the same as for any non-Christian, and I suspect it has to do with our concept of the Divine. If I really understand who God is, what his posture is toward me (grace!), how powerful, how loving, how perfect, how magnificent he is, then loving him occurs as a natural by-product of this knowledge. Unfortunately, most of the world doesn't have a conscious clue as to what his character is. And because of lack of knowledge, God isn't treasured.

One: In order for God to be treasured for who he is, we have to know who he is.

Sometimes my soul just needs a reminder of the truth about God's character. Occasionally I need to look at the complexity of creation and marvel at the Designer. Every day in my job as a surgeon, I'm reminded of the incredible detail and harmony present in the human body—100 trillion cells all working together as a complex unit. Or look outside.

> Light travels 5.87 trillion miles a year. Our solar system is 100,000 light years in diameter, about 587,000 trillion miles. It is one of about a million such galaxies in the optical range of our most powerful telescopes. In our galaxy there are more than 200 billion stars. The sun is only one of them, traveling in an orbit at 135 miles/second, taking 250

million years to complete a revolution around the
galaxy.[1]

Wow. I can't get my head around that. This is the Creator
whom we serve, the one who deserves our love. A God like that
is worthy of being the controlling passion of my life.

It's easy for me to point to the nonbeliever and see that a lack
of knowledge prevents God from being the focus of his love,
but how do I account for my own heart being sluggish in love
for my Heavenly Father? Have I not let misconceptions about
his motives toward me slip in and crowd out the truth? This
happens at a nearly imperceptible level. I'm moving through the
day, finding myself discouraged about negative circumstances,
perhaps allowing this to be manifested by short-temperedness
with my family or those around me. At that point, have I not
slipped into the lie that God is not acting on my behalf to bring
about his sovereign will? Have I not forgotten that he is all-
loving and all-knowing and that he has promised to finish the
work that he began in my life?

At that point it can be argued that the problem is not that
I do not know God's character but that I'm not believing it.
Regardless of the problem's root, I am functioning as if I don't
know his character or believe it is true. At the point of my need,
my discouragement over circumstances, I need to consciously
remind my pathetic, forgetful soul of the truth of God's character. This is the first step to reentering love with the Father.
As I dwell on the truth of his love and his character, I begin to
love him with my emotions (soul) and my will (heart). We can
argue that loving him with our soul, heart, and strength can
actually begin as we love him with our mind, searching out the
correct theology about him.

Proper knowledge presupposes exposure to the truth and the discipline to study it. A proper understanding of who God is means light needs to reach the dark places of our misconceptions. If my concept of God is that he is a stern taskmaster, a strict accountant of sins, just waiting to punish me when I'm out of line, I won't love him. If he is distant, cool, and uninterested in me, why should I care about him? If I think he delights in evil and orchestrates painful circumstances for his own amusement, the result in me will be malice, not love.

But this is not our God. Our Father is loving, relentlessly delighting in us as his cherished bride. Too often misconceptions cause us to stumble out of love.

The biggest single problem in the Christian church today is the failure to grasp who our glorious God is, and that makes it hard for us to love him. We listen to a myriad of other voices, but not his voice. We listen to our own heart, concentrating on our unworthiness, sin, and shortcomings rather than on the truth as it is presented in the Bible. The slide into unbelief about his love is sometimes subtle. A negative experience results in a flurry of negative thoughts about our lives. *I'll never live up to my own expectations, much less that of a perfect God. I'm a failure. A sinner. Unworthy. Unloved.* Soon we've slipped into depression and dryness of soul, and we're unable to hear the truth.

That's one reason that our souls need to hear the truth every day. Hourly I need to remind myself of my position as his beloved. Walking in the overflow of this truth results in refreshing splashes of love from my life into the lives of those around me.

Two: In order for God to be treasured, we have to believe the truth about his character.

For any truth to impact an individual to the point of causing a change in behavior, the individual has to believe the truth. This is problem number two. The truth that we've heard about God flows off the crusty ground of our hearts unabsorbed due to unbelief. Wondrous news cannot impact our souls if we don't believe. *Sure, I've heard the words, God loves me. But it's almost too good to be true.* We harbor secret doubts. *If he really loved me, my husband wouldn't have left. I wouldn't have gotten cancer. My boss would appreciate me.*

Oh, how quickly negative emotions and feelings can make us forget the truth. Elsewhere I've previously detailed the concept of "gospel debt,"[2] the spiritual equivalent to oxygen debt, a condition we've all experienced after heavy exercise. Our muscles find themselves in a state of low oxygen, so we breathe faster and our hearts race to make up the debt. Our muscles demand payment, and the currency is oxygen. When in gospel debt, I am functioning as if the cross of Christ—his death in my place, to pay for my sins—isn't fully sufficient to place me in right standing with the Father. I perform good works to tip the scales in my favor; or conversely, I excuse my sinfulness as somehow being something less distasteful, a white lie or a slipup, a mistake. Regardless, my soul is demanding payment, and the currency is grace.

The cure for finding myself out of love with Jesus is similar to the spiritual resuscitation I undergo for treatment of gospel debt, the ABC's that guide our therapy. I recognize a symptom, anxiety or discouragement perhaps. First I **acknowledge** my need. Then, I **believe** the gospel and the promises in it. And finally I spend time in **communion**, quietly spending time in his presence to allow the truth of the gospel to penetrate every area of my life. When I find myself out of love with God, I'm functioning in a gospel debt of sorts. I've allowed feelings, situations, or circumstances to crowd away the consciousness of the character of God and his loveliness. The cure is to believe again the promises of or the truth about God. As I stay in communion with him alone, my focus shifts from me to him (in view of the enormity of his greatness, all of my needs and even all of my accomplishments are nothing), and love is the result.

Believing the truth about God is really a gift. Without God reaching out toward us and enlightening us with faith, we would still be groping in darkness without him. And even now, as Christians, belief in his promises is still a gift. When we find ourselves functioning outside of love for Christ, in effect not believing the truth about his character, we should cry out like the man who asked Jesus to heal his sick child.

> Immediately the father of the child cried out and said, "I believe; help my unbelief!"
> —Mark 9:24

The third problem is really a subset of numbers 1 and 2. As a result of not really grasping an adequate knowledge of God's character or not believing it, we allow something else to slip into the top passion spot.

Three: I've allowed something else to become the controlling passion of my life.

I can't say it better than the prophet Jeremiah.

> Be appalled, O heavens, at this; be shocked, be utterly desolate, declares the LORD, for my people have committed two evils: they have forsaken me, the fountain of living waters, and hewed out cisterns for themselves, broken cisterns that can hold no water.
> —Jeremiah 2:12–13

This is exactly what we do when we allow something else to become our *numero uno*. We play in leaky wading pools, stagnant with green slime, oblivious to the abundant fountain available for continuous refreshing.

That's ridiculous, you say. And you're right. It's crazy to play in a stagnant, leaky pool when a waterfall is within reach. That's why Jeremiah used the language he used. It's appalling! Shocking! Unbelievable! So why do we do it?

I think it has to do with our wiring. God has designed us to allow only one thing into the top spot. Jesus explained it this way:

> "No one can serve two masters, for either he will hate the one and love the other, or he will be devoted to the one and despise the other. You cannot serve God and money."
>
> —Matthew 6:24

The apostle John drives it home.

> Do not love the world or the things in the world. If anyone loves the world, the love of the Father is not in him.
>
> —1 John 2:15

Ouch. And just in case you were wondering what "the world" is, he explains it so we can't misunderstand.

> For all that is in the world—the desires of the flesh and the desires of the eyes and pride in possessions— is not from the Father but is from the world.
>
> —1 John 2:16

Ouch again. Spend an hour with American television, and the competition for the top spot is unmistakable. Buy! Enjoy! Splurge! But the fulfillment from materialism is short-lived. Jesus called it "the deceitfulness of riches." Remember the Parable of the Sower?

> "As for what was sown among thorns, this is the one who hears the word, but the cares of the world and the deceitfulness of riches choke the word, and it proves unfruitful."
>
> —Matthew 13:22

In essence, love was sowed in our hearts by the Holy Spirit at our new birth. Allow me to return to my premise. Remember, I believe that love is what should and will define the Christian as long as it is given proper nourishment. It is that way by design. But just as DNA defines and determines a set path and behavior for individual cells, but that path can be thwarted by illness, so the seed of love that has been planted within us can falter and fail to yield fruit because of the competition—"cares" and "riches."

It is true that what you love will control you. And we are hard-wired to have only one top spot. So if God isn't in control, who is? The question could be rephrased: Whom or what do you love? Your car, house, investment portfolio? Your reputation, position, convenience, comfort?

Jeremiah has the correct response to those of us who answer honestly that we've turned away from the fountain to our cracked cisterns: Appalling!

Some of you recognize the competition for your heart's attention right away. You're not alone. We all suffer from yielding our heart's top spot to other lovers from time to time. And if you don't see it, pray that you will.

A solution begins with a knowledge of the fountain and believing it can satisfy and then turning away from our leaky wading pools and entering back into the waterfall of God's love.

Allowing the competition to control us is likely to lead to disaster. Which brings me back to my father's pale yellow Subaru.

The yellow Subaru galloped forward, unrestricted and un-controlled, gaining speed at the will of gravity. Fortunately, it traveled relatively straight. So it avoided the pond but slammed straight into a barn-like utility shed.

Not a pretty sight. And not such a good start to a promising dating relationship either. Looking back, I think that relationship was pretty much doomed from the beginning. Later my mother shared something with me that pretty much sealed the fate of my infatuation with the blue-eyed girl. I think it ranks right up there in the top five worries of young Mennonite men as they enter the dangerous game of courtship.

My mother smiled and let her hand rest gently on my shoulder. "You know she's your cousin, don't you?"

For Further Reflection

1. Do you agree that God's will for you can be summed up in loving him and loving your neighbors? Which of these do you find the most difficult? Why?

2. Does a limited knowledge of God hinder you from loving him with all your heart? What will you do to experience improvement in this area?

3. Do you truly believe that God loves you and cares about you, that he is a gracious God? Why or why not? How does the *acknowledgment—belief—communion* outline help here?

4. Has something else captured the top billing in your life that belongs only to God? What is it? What can you do to let God become your highest passion once again?

5. Do you love the world, as the apostle John defines *world*? Which phrase in 1 John 2:16 ("the desires of the flesh . . . the desires of the eyes . . . pride in possessions") most accurately describes your love affair with the godless world system? Specifically, what will you do to turn away from the world and to God?

Chapter Four

LOVING YOUR NEIGHBOR
WITH THE PURPLE PANTS

Spend fifteen minutes in an American shopping mall and you'll see how far people are willing to go to find acceptance within their peer group. I think it's part of the love-shaped void in all of us. If everybody else has a piece of metal shoved through his or her eyebrow, I want one too. I want to fit. I want to be loved.

I remember clothes shopping with my mom as she helped prepare me for the sixth grade. I could have enjoyed that quality time with my mother, except our goals were opposite, and opposite goals create tension. She wanted me to have school clothes that fit and would last as long as possible. I wanted to be doing anything except shopping for clothes. Come to think of it, I still shop for clothes with that attitude. Get in. Buy a pair of pants, usually the first one on the rack that pleases me, like the worn pair of khakis that I'm replacing, and get out.

Efficient. Fast. That's probably why my wife doesn't invite me shopping.

So when my mother found a pair of pants that I said would work, she did the practical thing and bought two pairs, so I could wear one while the other one was being washed. Do you recall what I told you about being brought up Mennonite? Remember the two mental boxes I had for categorizing everything into church or worldly? Well, clothes are particularly troublesome if you're worried about keeping separate from the world. In general the rules were, don't stand out; cover most of your skin. Now I wasn't brought up among the conservatives. Their wardrobe was particularly restricted: cape dresses for the women and plain coats for the men. My family wasn't like that, but nonetheless we were a bit fashion-challenged.

But when my mom and I went shopping for what I would wear to the sixth grade, I think I might have mixed up the mental boxes. I bought two pairs of corduroy pants that were two-toned: bright purple and light blue. The colors were laid out in a pattern so that the thigh of one leg was purple, and the other was blue. The lower legs were the same except for opposite coloring; if the thigh was purple, the lower leg was blue. You get the picture. It wasn't pretty.

In the early 1970s, Virginia was struggling with race issues. The way the city of Newport News handled it was by busing most of the middle-class kids from my neighborhood downtown to go to school with the kids from predominantly African-American neighborhoods. So I attended a fairly integrated class and had classmates with nicknames like Punchy and Globe. The way the downtown kids pronounced it, it always came out "Glo." I later learned that Globe had gotten his nickname because of the large size of his head. Kids can be cruel.

Anyway, with my purple and blue corduroys, I was set to attend a new school. Fifth grade and the blonde cousin of Paul McCartney were behind me. She'd moved on, probably with Kevin. I rode the bus downtown to a new school. I wanted to fit in. I had a love-shaped void.

So what happened? I arrived with my new pants, and the kids in my class laughed at *my shoes!* Globe pointed at my feet. "Where'd you get those butter cookies?" It seemed that the other parts of my wardrobe mattered little. At my new school, wearing Converse tennis shoes was the key to acceptance, and unfortunately my shoes were Keds or some other brand that ushered me to the outside of Cool Central.

Why tell that story now? Because love for your neighbor is the natural outflow of a life lived in love with God. And it starts with acceptance of others regardless of the color of their skin or the shoes they wear.

During a recent night on call, I was awakened by a phone call. It was 4 in the morning. *Who is calling at this hour?* I pressed the phone to my ear, my speech thickened by lips not yet fully awake. "Hello."

"Dr. Kraus, there's been a bus accident. We need you in casualty." Casualty is the African equivalent of the E.R.

A bus accident. A mass casualty. That's all we needed. Our mission hospital report from the night before was that we were already 6 percent over maximum capacity and that we were going to have to convert the chapel into space for more beds.

I put on a pair of surgical scrubs and walked up the dirt road to the hospital, wondering just what I'd find. Describing the scene in casualty as noisy, bloody, or confusing all fall short. It was crowded. Bleeding and mangled bodies everywhere. Every stretcher full. Other patients sitting in chairs and crying for attention.

Several patients were critical, and within the hour I was in surgery with the first one, a two-year-old with a severe scalp injury, trying to make sense of the puzzle of skin flaps peeled from his skull.

As I operated, his blood pressure sagged. My patient had lost so much blood, we were having trouble giving replacement intravenous fluid fast enough. Fortunately, we were able to keep him alive and support the blood pressure by giving him lots of saline (balanced salt solution) and eventually a blood transfusion.

In clinical situations when a patient has lost blood, our resuscitation volume is guided by a simple formula. We replace every unit of blood lost with three liters of salt solution. Why so much? Because most of the body is made up of fluid that is quickly distributed throughout all of the cells in an automatic sharing of fluids to keep the proper balance.

Two-thirds of the body's water is inside cells. One third is outside the cells, in the fluid around the cells or in the bloodstream. When a person bleeds, the cells send fluid into the bloodstream to keep everything balanced. Likewise, when we give fluid directly into the bloodstream, that fluid is quickly shared into every cell of the body, all one hundred trillion of them!

This give and take of water takes place by design. When the orders go out to compensate for a loss of blood or fluid, every cell does its part. When muscle cells have been injured in an accident, all of the body's cells contribute fluid to make up for the losses. Liver cells don't ask, "Who is going to benefit from this donation of my fluid?" and hold out only to donate when other liver cells are in need.

This occurs at an amazing rate. Referring to red blood cells as an example, a popular medical physiology book teaches us:

> Enough water ordinarily diffuses in each direction
> through the red cell membrane per second to equal

about *100 times the volume of the cell itself.* Yet, normally, the amount that diffuses in the two directions is balanced so precisely that zero *net* movement of water occurs.[1]

The free give-and-take of fluid from each cell is a picture of the way love is to be shared among individual members of Christ's body. Constantly. By design.

Did you ever notice that every time we see the metaphor of the body of Christ in the Bible, it is followed immediately by a discussion about or a reference to love? Look at 1 Corinthians 13, the chapter devoted to a description of *agape* love. What precedes it? A discussion about the body of Christ and its individual members and functions. Romans 12:4–8 is another beautiful passage about the body of Christ. A simple phrase follows in verse 9: "Let love be genuine." And following a discussion for the reasons for the differing offices of apostles, prophets, pastors, and teachers, Paul concludes:

> Rather, speaking the truth in love, we are to grow up in every way into him who is the head, into Christ, from whom the whole body, joined and held together by every joint with which it is equipped, when each part is working properly, makes the body grow so that it builds itself up in love.
>
> —Ephesians 4:15–16

The link is there for a reason. Undeniably. Love is to be the natural outflow of the body of Christ, with each member contributing as it should. Of course, for that to happen, individual cells need to be healthy, and we'll get to a discussion of that later. In Chapter One, we saw that love is to be the defining, dominant characteristic of the body of Christ, the evidence of our discipleship to a world longing for love. What I'd like you to see from a closer inspection of the body of Christ metaphor is that this flow of love isn't something that's contrived or forced. Cells within the human body normally experience the give-and-take that is necessary for health and vitality. Likewise, healthy members of the body of Christ will love each other as a natural result of the transformation of God's Spirit working within them.

A key in the verses above is the prepositional phrase, "when each part is working properly." For individual cells in the body to be healthy and work properly there must be maintenance. Liberal amounts of oxygen, appropriate nutrition, plenty of water, sleep, moderate exercise, and appropriate protection from the environment are the basic needs of the human body. Sometimes, even when all of these are maintained, the health of the body is attacked by illness such as cancer or infection.

Love, the defining quality of the body of Christ, occurs naturally as a consequence of well-being.

My point is that when things are as they should be, each cell functions in a benevolent way, assuring the health of the entire organism. But when the basics are ignored, all bets are off. If the body is healthy, we love!

Acting with benevolence is the essence of love. Dallas Willard, professor and philosopher, helps us with a definition.

> And first, what exactly is love? It is *will to good* or "bene-volence." We love something or someone when we promote its good for its own sake. Love's contrary is malice, and its simple absence is indifference. Its normal accompaniment is delight, but a twisted soul may delight in evil and take no pleasure in good.
>
> Love is not the same thing as desire, for I may desire something without even wishing it well, much less

willing its good. I might desire a chocolate ice cream cone, for example, but I do not wish it well; I wish to eat it. This is the difference between lust (mere desire) and love, as between a man and a woman. Desire and love are, of course, compatible when desire is ruled by love; but most people today would, unfortunately, not even know the difference between them. Hence, in our world, love constantly falls prey to lust. That is a major part of the deep sickness of contemporary life. By contrast, what characterizes the deepest essence of God is love—that is, will to good.[2]

Jesus' commands that we are to love God above all but also one another, our neighbors, and even our enemies can appear outrageous at first glance. *Come on, get real,* we think. *He can't mean my neighbor.* A point worth reemphasizing is that just as there are many naturally occurring functions in the healthy human body, so love is to be the natural fruit of the healthy body of Christ. So yes, Jesus is quite serious, but his command is not meant to result in our despair. He's not asking the impossible. He's only telling us what will happen if we submit to the disciplines that result in our spiritual maturity, disciplines that keep us abiding in him. It will happen naturally. Surely.

What the body of Christ metaphor can help us understand is that although many functions of the body occur naturally, maintenance is essential. That's where we'll go in subsequent chapters. For now I want to look a bit more closely at just what this love looks like.

Looking at the body of Christ metaphor, we first see the obvious: there is one body with many members, each individually equipped to perform a certain function designed to enhance the whole. A liver cell functions differently than a muscle cell. A skin cell performs differently than a thyroid cell *by design.* Each cell performs a specialized task or group of tasks according to its individual calling. The muscle cell performs more efficiently if the liver cell is doing one of its many jobs—releasing needed glucose into the bloodstream for uptake by exercising muscles. At the core of each of these cells is the same DNA. But under the influence of their individual specialization, the message from the DNA is expressed a bit differently. Some specialized molecules are only made by thyroid cells—that is, thyroid hormone. Now, the information allowing a cell to make thyroid hormone is stored within the same DNA that resides in every cell. But because of specialization, only thyroid cells are able to make thyroid hormone, a hormone that is ultimately needed by the rest of the body to regulate the speed of metabolism.

What's my point? Simply that although the same love of God has been poured into our hearts and defines us as members of Christ's body, that love will be expressed in different ways depending on whether we are liver cells, thyroid cells, or skin cells in the body of Christ. Perhaps this seems to go without saying, but the effect of understanding this simple truth is our liberation. I am free to be whatever God calls me to be. I don't need to fear that I can't love. Fear is the result of misunderstanding just what love looks like. Perhaps I look around, anxious that I won't be able to generate the right love feelings. Hogwash. Biblical love is so much more.

With the appropriate body maintenance, you will express God's love in a way that is unique to your individual calling.

If my understanding of love is too narrow—that is, if I've fallen prey to the influences of Hollywood on my thinking about love—I'll be discouraged. I can't fill my heart with the fluffy, sweet, syrupy feelings of desire toward my neighbor that characterizes only one aspect of love. I believe that Willard's definition is key: love "is *will to good* or 'bene-volence.' We love something or someone when we promote its good for its own sake."[3] The way a liver cell acts benevolently toward its neighbors looks differently than the love that is expressed by a thyroid cell.

Don't despair if you can't seem to whip up the right kind of emotions. *Agape* love is so much more than emotion. The way you love your neighbor will look different than the way others love neighbors based on your individual gifts. According to 1 Corinthians 12:11, we are all "empowered by one and the same Spirit, who apportions to each one individually as he wills."

What does this love look like? Remember the words of Jesus.

> "'For I was hungry and you gave me food, I was thirsty and you gave me drink, I was a stranger and you welcomed me, I was naked and you clothed me, I was sick and you visited me, I was in prison and you came to me. . . . Truly, I say to you, as you did it to one of the least of these my brothers, you did it to me.'"
>
> —Matthew 25:35–36, 40

A liver cell cannot decide to be a thyroid cell. A liver cell will perform comfortably and efficiently as a liver cell because it has been designed to do exactly the job that it performs. And, silly as it sounds, liver cells do not despair if they cannot benefit the whole body the same way a thyroid cell can.

> But as it is, God arranged the members in the body, each one of them, as he chose. If all were a single member, where would the body be? As it is, there are many parts, yet one body.
>
> —1 Corinthians 12:18–20

Here's the bottom line. God designed you to receive love, shaped you with a love-shaped void that only he can fill, intended for your life to be characterized by love, and designed you in a unique way to love the others around you.

The main thing isn't that you memorize Scripture, share your faith, preach three-point sermons that are admired by everyone, pray regularly, or attend a church service every Sunday. The main thing isn't that you give generously to the poor or donate your time to a soup kitchen. The main thing is love. Now love may include all those things, but unless these activities are manifestations of love, they are pointless. Nothing. The cracked cymbal syndrome (see 1 Corinthians 13:1).

God has called pastors, teachers, apostles, and prophets but also a myriad of others—plumbers, carpenters, taxi drivers, homemakers, artists, novelists, architects, engineers, and thousands of others. The love coming from each of them may look different, but it will all have the same core, a will for good toward the recipients.

Can mowing the grass be love? Sure. Writing a note of encouragement? Absolutely. So can plumbing, carpentry, poetry, accounting, giving, singing, designing jeans, driving a cab, and baking lasagna. What are your individual gifts? Each of them can be and should be used as a manifestation of God's love to the world around you. Our Hollywood concept of love has limited our appreciation of the many, many ways that love can be expressed. In short, the benevolence of love is unlimited in presentation but will always have as a central component the performance of good toward another without selfish motive. A familiar Bible passage helps us understand what love is and is not:

> Love is patient and kind; love does not envy or boast;
> it is not arrogant or rude. It does not insist on its
> own way; it is not irritable or resentful; it does not

rejoice at wrongdoing, but rejoices with the truth. Love bears all things, believes all things, hopes all things, endures all things.

—1 Corinthians 13:4–7

I believe that with appropriate nutrition, individual cells have no choice but to mature and perform the functions they were designed to perform. Likewise each of us, when we expose ourselves to the disciplines of discipleship (the proper nutrition, so to speak), will *naturally* begin to love those around us.

That's the way we're designed.

And that is liberating news.

Love! That's an order!

It almost goes without saying that the human body acts under direct instruction from the brain. When I picked up my laptop to begin working, my fingers did not begin to worry, *What if I can't think of what to write?* When I don a pair of surgical gloves to repair a laceration, my hands are simply functioning under the will of my brain. My hands don't need to originate the movements necessary to perform the will of the brain.

It sounds almost silly to say it that way, doesn't it? Of course the hands obey the brain.

That should be liberating news, don't you think?

We are called the body of Christ, not the brain of Christ. Let's look again at what the head is guiding us to do. An examination of Scripture reveals numerous imperatives that are clear instructions for us to follow. I know of no other instruction that Jesus left us that is given in such strong language. As I was working on this, I quickly counted twelve verses that use the word "command," "commanded," or "commandment" when it refers to the task of loving (Matthew 22:36, 38, 40; Mark 12:28, 31; John 13:34; 15:12, 17; 1 John 3:23; 4:21; 2 John 5–6).

Perhaps we should consider why this same forceful language isn't used for other religious activities—witnessing, praying, or giving, for example.

Or is it possible that love looks like each of those things when expressed through different members of the body? Or maybe love is the main thing and without it, everything else falls flat on the sidewalk of failure. Fulfillment of the Great Commission is every Christian's calling. Being an evangelist isn't. Loving is every Christian's calling. And if we make love our aim, I think we'll see the Great Commission fulfilled in the process.

A soldier doesn't vacillate back and forth, wondering if an order is to be carried out or not. A command is simply carried out; orders are followed. The infantryman in battle does not think of the special circumstances that make the order impractical or inapplicable. Again obedience follows.

But sometimes I treat Jesus' commands to love just like that. *Certainly God would make an exception in my special case. No one could love a neighbor who . . .*

Such a line of excuses is appalling. No faithful soldier behaves in this way.

I love the way Christ dealt with the lawyer in Luke 10. When told he needed to love his neighbor, the first thing the attorney did was look for a loophole. "And who is my neighbor?" (Luke 10:29b).

Look closely at Jesus' answer. He used a great tactic. He told a story, and in the end he turned the question around:

> "Which of these three, do you think, proved to be a neighbor to the man who fell among the robbers?"
>
> —Luke 10:36

To whom are we to be neighbors? A friend of mine, longtime medical missionary Robert Congdon, says the answer is obvious by implication: "Whoever God puts in your path."

During my years in Africa, I have seen plenty of examples of what I call second-mile grace, love that goes beyond normal sacrifice to help the suffering whom God has placed in our path. Missionary surgeons operate and then turn around and donate their own blood for transfusion to the patients they've just performed surgery on. I know of two surgeons who operated on abandoned children and then went through the lengthy process of adoption to bring those children into their families.

Practically, how do you love your neighbor when you just plain don't feel like it? Presbyterian Church of America pastor Ken Aldrich has an answer: "You just love them." *What? I just said I didn't feel like it.* It doesn't matter. Once we've gotten over the fact that love isn't some fluffy emotion, it's easy to see how it works. When we obey and reach out to assist our neighbors (that is, anyone whom God puts in our path), we will find that enjoyment of the act follows. The caboose is pulled along behind the steam engine of obedience and the coal car of faith. We obey and then need to beg God to bring our heart along. Obedience in and of itself is a start and doesn't guarantee heart transformation. For that, we need the power of the Holy Spirit to quicken us with new life.

In subsequent chapters I want to go a bit deeper into the metaphor of the church being the body of Christ. Specifically, we need to see that the human body obeys the head most efficiently when all of the automatic functions are in proper working order.

What does a body do automatically? It hungers for food when it needs nourishment, thirsts when it is dehydrated, sleeps when it needs rest, and breathes when it needs oxygen. Without doing those things, the body suffers, illness ensues, and carrying out the commands of the head becomes difficult or impossible. Without paying attention to these basic needs, the body weakens into a malnourished, infection-prone condition in need of a physician's house call.

Maybe some of these "automatics" are malfunctioning in the body of Christ today.

Is this why we're missing *the main thing*?

Is this why I struggle to love?

For Further Reflection

1. What is the connection between the body of Christ (the church) and love? How does this work out in specific practical ways?

2. What are the differences between love, desire, and lust? What is the significance of this?

3. What is the importance of the church's being one body but many members spiritually? Why does God's love in the church not always look the same?

4. "*Agape* love is so much more than emotion." Do you agree or disagree? Why? If that statement is true, what is *agape* comprised of other than emotion?

5. Is love really more than fluffy emotion? How can we love others when we don't feel loving?

Part Two

Basic Body of Christ
Health Maintenance

Chapter Five

ANOREXIA

I t's a scenario played out over and over in emergency rooms across the world. A young child suspected of having appendicitis awaits the opinion of the on-call surgeon. The surgeon always begins the same way—talking to the patient, asking the parents about the symptoms, stepping down the decision pathway toward a conclusion. To cut or not to cut? Is an operation needed?

The experienced surgeon attempts to put the patient at ease, asking about the tattered stuffed animal clenched tightly by the young girl. He gently touches the animal's head. "I had a monkey like this once. His name was Bobo. What's your friend's name?"

The patient looks up with wide eyes. "Samson."

The surgeon smiles. "Strong name," he says. "What does Samson like to eat?"

"Bananas."

"I like bananas too." He gently rocks the stretcher while the patient is distracted, watching for a reaction.

The face of the little patient tightens in a grimace.

The surgeon continues. "What's your favorite food, Kristy?"

The patient whimpers, "Pizza."

"Wow," he responds. "Me too. If I could get a pizza, your very favorite kind, would you like to have some now?"

The patient is curled up, lying on her side. "No," she cries. "I'm not hungry."

The surgeon nods. *Could be appendicitis.*

The patient's loss of appetite is a common symptom that may or may not reflect a serious underlying problem. So why ask about it? Because the absence of the symptom—that is, if the patient has a healthy appetite—is almost never associated with appendicitis. If the patient says he or she is hungry, the surgeon had better think of another diagnosis.

In medical lingo, we use the word *anorexia* for loss of appetite. This is not to be confused with anorexia nervosa, the pathologic illness in which there are associated body image problems and an overwhelming feeling of not being thin enough. If a patient has anorexia, that doesn't point to a specific diagnosis, but the absence usually means that the sudden onset of appendicitis (acute appendicitis) is not present.

If only things were so straightforward in Africa . . .

I was called into the operating theatre by an orthopedic (bone) specialist. On the table in front of us was a patient, already under anesthesia and undergoing surgery. She had developed a chronic drainage from over the prominence of the wing of her right pelvic bone. I examined her X-ray and agreed. There seemed to be an area of the bone eaten away by infection. Osteomyelitis or bone infection occurs commonly in Kenya. The bone surgeon was planning to follow the draining sinus, dissecting to the bone and removing the damaged tissue to allow healing. There was only one problem. When he examined the bone, it appeared normal. I scrubbed in, examined the patient, and helped the bone surgeon follow the drainage pathway deep into the muscles of the flank where it seemed to end. Unprepared to go further, we collected some drainage for culture and ended the operation.

A few days later, I received the culture result. The drainage contained a bacteria commonly found in the gastrointestinal tract, not a bug commonly associated with bone infections. I performed exploratory surgery, opening the abdomen, and found that the appendix had ruptured, sealing itself off into the muscles of the right flank. The infection had smoldered, leaking intestinal contents into the soft tissue and creeping along a meandering path until it popped through the skin about six inches from the perforation site.

Appendicitis presenting in this fashion is almost unheard of in the United States. But here in Kenya, where availability of treatment or lack of money or ignorance or all three predominate, the unusual is usual.

But almost all cases begin with anorexia.

Spiritual anorexia, or lack of spiritual hunger, is common inside and outside the church today.

In our examination of the metaphor of the body of Christ, our focus is on gaining an understanding of how the body, when it is healthy, will perform what it has been designed to do—that is, love naturally. By design, the body does some things that maintain health. Like hunger and thirst. And breathing. Automatically. The functions or desires we are born with and don't have to learn. Functions that, when they are absent, may signal trouble—a spiritual appendicitis, you might say.

Consider the sensation of hunger. Ask any new mother. After a few days of life it seems that all newborn babies do is eat, sleep, and poop. And when they want to eat, they let you know loudly and clearly!

And not just once a day or three meals a day like a reasonable adult, but without respect to the clock. Day and night their mantra is the same as the advertising slogan for the dairy association. "Got milk?"

Within a few months of writing this, I'm going to be the father of three teenaged sons. Teenage boys are many things. Loud. Active. Fun. Sometimes forgetful of a schoolbook or a school assignment. But never, ever has one of my teenagers laid down to sleep at night and thought, *I forgot to eat today. All day long. No breakfast, lunch, dinner, or snack. I just didn't think about it.*

Crazy idea. It's even more ludicrous to imagine going a week without eating just because other activities crowded eating into an ignored corner.

But there are nights I lie down to sleep and remember that my Bible remained unopened all day long.

The apostle Peter says that our desire for the Word of God should mimic a baby's desire for milk.

> Like newborn infants, long for the pure spiritual milk, that by it you may grow up into salvation—if indeed you have tasted that the Lord is good.
>
> —1 Peter 2:2–3

This convicts me. Do I long for the Word of God the way a baby does for milk? When was the last time I woke up at night, hungry for a word from God, and cried out to my Heavenly Father to feed my soul?

Miss a meal, and your stomach will let you know. Miss a few, and the body begins to weaken. Eventually, without food, the body begins to chew up its own muscle for energy. Starvation ensues. The body becomes infection prone, unable to combat viruses or pathologic bacteria. Eventually the body avoids movement altogether. Picture the children with bellies bloated with fluid, the ones the relief organizations use to prick our consciences to motivate us to give.

Take a moment to consider your spiritual nutritional fitness. Healthy? Listless and dragging from a missed meal or two? Or bedridden-ineffective from months of starvation?

It is impossible for a healthy individual to go without food for long periods without feeling hungry. I believe that as long as the body of Christ is healthy, we will experience spiritual hunger. If we don't, our spiritual anorexia should prompt an examination, looking for the underlying soul illness. Prolonged spiritual anorexia leads to malnutrition.

God points to a state of hunger as a coveted position. It is a blessed condition, a state of the soul that will certainly be rewarded.

> Let them thank the LORD for his steadfast love, for his wondrous works to the children of man! For he satisfies the longing soul, and the hungry soul he fills with good things.
> —Psalm 107:8–9

> "Blessed are those who hunger and thirst for righteousness, for they shall be satisfied."
> —Matthew 5:6

Jesus said to them, "I am the bread of life; whoever
comes to me shall not hunger, and whoever believes
in me shall never thirst."

—John 6:35

"Do not labor for the food that perishes, but for the
food that endures to eternal life."

—John 6:27

Malnutrition is common in sub-Sahara Africa. War, government corruption, poverty, drought, and natural disasters all
combine to set the stage for widespread starvation. A spiritual
equivalent is easy to see. But in America, inside the Christian
church, the problem isn't a lack of available nutrition. It's starvation in the face of plenty, anorexia at Grandma's table of
Thanksgiving abundance.

How can this be? How can we go weeks without opening
our Bibles? Thousands of spiritually malnourished Christians
limp into weekly services for their only feeding during a seven-
day fast. They gorge for a few minutes (and it better not be
more than twenty or thirty or the congregation won't tolerate
it) each Sunday and starve the rest of the week. And yet this is
starvation without a symptom. We just aren't hungry anymore.
Where does this anorexia come from?

It's an interesting study to look at the complexities of human
appetite. There are several phases, including the stimulation of
our hunger just by the pleasing aroma of food. We walk into
a bakery, and our mouths begin to salivate.

Some of us need to remind our souls of the satisfaction of
feasting on God and his Word to stimulate our appetites. The
aroma of food to whet our appetites is like worship in that it
prepares our hearts to receive God's Word.

For others, the problems run deeper than needing an appetite stimulant. We're suffering from spiritual illnesses, and our anorexia is only one of a myriad of symptoms. We'll look at a few common maladies and their solutions in later chapters.

Remember sneaking to the cookie jar before dinner? Get caught and your mother would likely warn, "You're going to spoil your appetite!"

Some of us have been feasting on substitute loves, when God has designed us to function in a certain way only when we've found him to be the source of satisfaction and life. And our spiritual appetite has been spoiled.

For others, the symptoms of anorexia have grown from a hardening of their hearts by sin's deceit.

By design, the body of Christ was created to love. But widespread anorexia has robbed the church of health and threatens our ability to function as intended.

From a standpoint of pathophysiology, anorexia can be protective of the whole. Consider appendicitis or other significant gastrointestinal disorders. The intestines, normally active and squeezing their contents happily downstream, are now paralyzed by infection or inflammation. Eating under those circumstances would load up an already backed up system, resulting in nausea and vomiting. If a person has a perforated stomach ulcer, the accompanying anorexia protects the patient from eating more, an act that would cause additional leakage of the stomach's contents into the abdominal cavity.

In those situations, the intestinal tract is not prepared to receive. There are times when our souls are unprepared for hearing God. Perhaps that is an anorexia of sorts. This is why it is important to prepare the ground for the seed of the Word, so it can take root and bear fruit.

> Sow for yourselves righteousness; reap steadfast love;
> break up your fallow ground, for it is the time to seek
> the LORD, that he may come and rain righteousness
> upon you.
>
> —Hosea 10:12

As a surgeon, I am treatment-oriented, and like most surgeons, I enjoy the instant gratification of seeing results of my work, good or bad, right away. So, what is the treatment for spiritual anorexia? The answer is dependent on the myriad of underlying causes. Almost all of them begin with recognition of the problem and repentance.

> *God, I'm starving, and I'm not even hungry. Bring me to the place where I can savor the aroma of your grace. Stimulate my desire for you. Help me see where I have substituted other food when I should have been feasting at your table.*

In the end, eating is a willful act made in response to our hunger.

In a healthy condition, a hearty appetite results. But in order to maintain health, something willful has to take place: we have to eat! It may seem obvious, but an actual lack of feeding, not a lack of appetite, is the problem for so many Christians. Some actually do eat, but their diet is unbalanced, and consequently they remain malnourished and ineffective, unable to love.

Just as God designed our physical bodies to need specific nutrients for survival and fitness, so he has created us as spiritual beings to need balanced spiritual nutrition for fitness. Our physical bodies need amino acids, the building blocks of protein, carbohydrates for energy, essential fatty acids, vitamins, minerals, and plenty of water. Our spiritual food must come from feasting on Christ himself, through a balanced consumption of every section of God's Word.

Physical well-being comes from daily, regular input. The next time you are bored at the breakfast table, read the side of a cereal box. Read the column of listed nutrients and the percentage of the *adult daily requirement* for each. Water-soluble vitamins have to be consumed every day because they can't be stored. Energy in the form of calories must be consumed daily to keep the machinery of the body fueled.

Likewise, we need organized, balanced, *daily* input of the Scriptures for proper spiritual health. Remember, manna was provided for the Israelites in the wilderness each day, and attempts to store it overnight resulted in food that was spoiled, unsuitable for consumption.

We had a rule during general surgery residency: Eat when you can, and sleep when you can, because you never know when the next opportunity might (or might not) arise. As members of the body of Christ, we would do well to have a similar attitude.

Some of us wish this was effortless. It's not. It takes the dreaded *d* word: *discipline*. Intentional. Planned. Exposure that isn't rushed. The apostle John says it this way:

> . . . if we love one another, God abides in us and his love is perfected in us.
>
> —1 John 4:12

And Jesus said:

> "Abide in me, and I in you. As the branch cannot bear fruit by itself, unless it abides in the vine, neither can you, unless you abide in me. I am the vine; you are the branches. Whoever abides in me and I

in him, he it is that bears much fruit, for apart from
me you can do nothing."

—John 15:4–5

The apostle John adds:

So we have come to know and to believe the love that
God has for us. God is love, and whoever abides in
love abides in God, and God abides in him.

—1 John 4:16

Love results from abiding in Christ, abiding in his love. Okay,
but practically what does this mean?

Abiding means taking time. Time spent in silence. Time spent
in worship. Time spent in meditative reading of Holy Scripture.
Abiding means walking in the constant awareness of his love for
you, daily reviewing, nourishing your soul with the truth of his
Word and encouraging your mind about his passion for you.

African culture has something to teach the rest of us about
the value of time. Here relationships take priority over schedules. We rarely begin a conversation here without first asking
about the well-being of a person's family. There is no rush to
the point here.

The most common mode of transportation in Kenya is the
matatu. A matatu is a van, usually holding fourteen passengers.
(Before passage of the most recent Kenyan law limiting the
number of passengers, the joke was often heard, "How many
Kenyans fit into a matatu? One more!") The backs of these ve-
hicles are often painted with individual slogans, messages unique
to the matatu owner and expressing his personal philosophy of
life. One said, "Time is money . . . so take your time!"

Come again? In the West, we would say, "Time is money,
so hurry up!"

Jesus invites us to come and dine. Sit, study, meditate, pray. Don't cram it down in a hurry just to check it off the to-do list.

Like the little patient with appendicitis, we all have our favorite foods. Perhaps we have a favorite Scripture passage we turn to over and over. That's wonderful. But be sure to study deeply, sampling from all of the Word to ensure balanced nutrition. That's one way to guarantee a life of love.

For Further Reflection

1. Is spiritual anorexia common in the church today? How does this manifest itself among Christians? In your life?

2. Do you long for God's Word the way a baby longs for milk? Why or why not?

3. Do you primarily feed on Scripture only in church on Sunday or also during the week? If the former, how is that affecting you spiritually? Will you determine right now to allow (or continue to allow) the Word to nourish you day by day?

4. "Some of us have been feasting on substitute loves, when God has designed us to function in a certain way only when we've found him to be the source of satisfaction and life. And our spiritual appetite has been spoiled." Do these words describe you? On what substitute loves have you been feeding?

5. What does it mean to you to abide in Christ, to abide in his love? What keeps you from doing this? Are these reasons or excuses? What can you do practically to abide in God's love?

Chapter Six

SPIRITUAL INSOMNIA

When I was in surgical training, we joked about the three rules that would help us survive. One: eat when you can. Two: sleep when you can. Three: don't mess with the pancreas.

Before laws restricting the number of hours a resident can spend on-call, the hours a doctor in training spent at the hospital could get a little extreme. Because there were usually only two interns on the cardiothoracic surgery service, it meant every other night call, in-hospital, to cover the needs of the open-heart patients. (Open-heart patients were the ones who underwent operations on the heart and utilized cardiopulmonary bypass, so that the heart could be arrested or stilled during the procedure so it could be operated on in a resting condition.) During Christmastime, in order to get a few nights off, the interns got creative in trading call nights. Our bosses didn't care as long as the service was covered 24/7 by an in-house intern.

So Dr. Kowalski, the other intern on the service, took off a week while I lived at the hospital, and he stayed while I took off a week. Good plan as long as you get some sleep, right?

I realize this sounds a bit like the parent who, back in his or her day had to walk six miles to school, in the snow, without shoes, uphill *both ways*, but I'm not making this up. I literally spent eight days in a row in the hospital without leaving, just so I could get some time off with my family at Christmas.

I don't remember it being so bad now. Perhaps the years have dulled my memory. My wife might feel differently. I do remember that she had a minor car accident and had plenty of time to get the car fixed before I ever saw it. She brought a picture of the car to the hospital for me to see. "Here's what it looked like," she said, holding up a picture. "But don't worry, I took the car to the body shop, and it's been fixed."

Eating wasn't so bad. I took meals in the cafeteria for lunches. Often my wife would bring something from home for supper, and we would eat together in the residents' lounge.

Sleeping meant grabbing z's in the call room at night in between pages from the nurses or new patients or whatever patient-problem-fires needed dousing.

There were many call nights with interrupted sleep. And when sleep deprivation demanded it, we crashed wherever and whenever we could.

Funny things happen during sleep deprivation. Thinking becomes slow. Response times are increased. Mental sharpness declines. The frequency of accidents increases. The brain sends out a constant message: *Leave me alone. I just need rest!* Pretty soon nothing else matters. The body in need of sleep can rest almost anywhere. *Just let me lie down on this counter for a minute.*

Turn out the lights in a conference room to show a few slides, and the interns are the first to yield their eyelids to the luxury of rest.

All bodies need sleep to maintain proper health. Without it, everything will unravel into inefficiency.

And do I need to point out that we're designed to need sleep in a *regular* cycle?

The Alarm Clock Generation

I once heard author and psychiatrist Paul Meier proclaim, "If you wake up to an alarm clock in the morning, you're out of God's will." He was speaking to a roomful of type A physicians at a Focus on the Family medical conference, and immediately he had our attention because all of us were setting our alarm clocks so we could drag ourselves out of bed in the morning!

To the alarm clock generation, his proclamation seems extreme. But is it?

God designed us to need sleep, designed sleep to come at regular intervals, and organized the body to function efficiently only with the renewal that comes from sleep. So if we are waking from sleep unnaturally, it is assumed we aren't getting enough.

In fact, current research indicates that sleep occurs, not passively as once was thought, but actively, by messages sent out from areas in the brain stem to the brain's cortex. This has been shown in animal studies where it has been observed that the brain's cortex will never sleep if input from the brain stem is severed.[1] (Of course, this is a condition inconsistent with human life!)

Rest or Else!

When the Bible uses the body of Christ as a metaphor for the church, we can conclude that efficient function (love) demands proper health maintenance. In the last chapter we looked at our need for spiritual nutrition. Now we turn our attention to our need for appropriate rest.

We see how important this must be to God when we read the Old Testament command.

> Six days shall work be done, but the seventh day is a Sabbath of solemn rest, holy to the LORD. Whoever does any work on the Sabbath day shall be put to death.
>
> —Exodus 31:15

Death? Yes. A severe consequence for violation of an injunction to rest! Get the idea? This is essential, critical stuff.

Please realize that I'm not trying to unload a legalist dump truck onto your backs. I'm just trying to help you see how important regular times of rest are *by God's design.*

One of my favorite passages of Scripture is found in Matthew.

> "Come to me, all who labor and are heavy laden, and I will give you rest. Take my yoke upon you, and learn from me, for I am gentle and lowly in heart, and you will find rest for your souls. For my yoke is easy, and my burden is light."
>
> —Matthew 11:28–30

"Come and find rest." Pretty straightforward, don't you think? But so many of us function as if he said, "Come unto me, and I'll put you to work. Take my yoke upon you, for I am a stern taskmaster, and you will find weariness for your souls. For my yoke is hard, and my burden is heavy."

The word translated "rest" in verse 28 is also translated "refresh" or "refreshed" in other verses, such as these verses in Philemon:

> For I have derived much joy and comfort from your love, my brother, because the hearts of the saints have been refreshed through you.
>
> —v. 7

> Yes, brother, I want some benefit from you in the Lord. Refresh my heart in Christ.
>
> —v. 20

Come to Christ to find rest. This doesn't just imply ceasing from labor. Come for soul refreshment.

A Lesson from the Thyroid Gland

Nearly every week in my surgical clinic, I see yet another patient with a runaway metabolism problem. With eyes bulging, heart racing, and neck swollen with a disobedient thyroid, the patient's appearance is not easy to forget. The condition is known as Graves' disease, a disease of the thyroid gland, which is normally small and nestled on both sides of your windpipe. The thyroid gland is responsible for the rate of all of the body's metabolism. If it is underactive, we gain weight, our skin dries out, and we get tired and constipated. If it is overactive, our heart gallops at a dangerous pace, and we feel jittery and hot when everyone else around us is comfortable.

The thyroid function is determined by the brain and utilizes an efficient negative feedback loop to turn on or shut off. It works like this. The thyroid produces thyroid hormone, the wonderful molecule that tells every cell to "speed up." If there is not enough thyroid hormone circulating in the bloodstream, the brain (specifically the pituitary gland at the base of the brain) sends a stimulating message to the thyroid gland: "We don't have enough thyroid hormone! Speed up production." Conversely, when enough thyroid hormone is in circulation, the pituitary gland stops sending the message to the thyroid, and thyroid hormone production is shut off.

Not so in Graves' disease, where the thyroid gland enlarges and stops listening to the messages sent by the brain. Even in the presence of adequate amounts of circulating thyroid hormone, the thyroid gland continues to pump out thyroid hormone, sending a message to every cell in the body (including itself): "Speed up production; work harder!"

In the Graves' disease patient, the thyroid gland sends the "work harder" message to the body's detriment. The heart is told to "beat faster, beat faster," until it begins to fail, unable to keep up with the demands of the strict taskmaster thyroid gland. The patient tires, and blood backs up into the lungs, producing a wet cough, low blood oxygen, and eventual death.

The message from the physical body is clear. Overworking the system can be deadly! By design, the body's metabolic rate is under direct influence of the brain. When the brain says, "rest," the body obeys.

Likewise, we need to listen to the gentle urgings of the Holy Spirit to get away and rest.

The example of Christ pulling away from the crowds to be alone with his Father should be example enough. But rest seems to be a low priority in a task-accomplishment-oriented society. Time alone with no agenda is frowned upon by a culture bent on goals and performance.

I'm a bit type A, so rest is something I need to work at! It helps to remember that we are the hands or feet and not the head. It is Christ's work, and we are only channels.

Spiritual insomnia occurs when busyness for God takes the place of God's business.

When working for God starts crowding out needed rest, spiritual insomnia is the result. Look at many American Christian congregations, and you'll likely find overworked leaders suffering this malady. By God's design, leaders are to be equippers, assisting all of the members to do ministry (love!) rather than the all too common scenario of the "professional" minister doing all the work.

Spiritual insomnia is a love-buster! When we're overworked and in need of refreshment, unexpected ministry opportunities are inconveniences instead of chances to be channels of our Father's love.

Treatment is tailored to the individual. Some of us need to learn to say no. All of us need to schedule margins in our lives. Regular, scheduled rest and reflection are as important to our spiritual health as regular sleep is to physical well-being.

During infancy and the teen years, extra sleep is needed because those are times of growth spurts and rapid development. Likewise, when we are experiencing times of extra spiritual growth, such as the deepening times of trials or special study, we need to be especially careful to schedule additional downtime, time alone before our Heavenly Lover with no agenda.

If I resent the workload, you can be sure love won't shine through.

If your life is anything like mine, finding regular downtime might be a battle. With every turn it seems there are more demands for our time, more opportunities for ministry.

When we return home to the U.S., we are struck by how American culture has swept so many Christians into a frantic vortex of activity. Children are shuttled from piano to soccer to play practice to youth group activities to karate and more. Parents feel obligated to expose their children to every available learning opportunity, while pursuing personal careers, doing volunteer work, and going to the gym. And then, of course, there's e-mail, the wonderful communication tool that sometimes adds another layer of business to the day. Outside ministry opportunities are not only turned down—they are just plain resented.

I sit back in wonder. *Maybe Africa has another lesson to teach us. Slow down. Value relationships over accomplishments.* If we're feeling stressed-out about our schedule, perhaps we should escape for a few days of silent retreat and give serious thought about each item that stretches us thin. It's possible that some of our busyness is culture-directed rather than Holy Spirit-directed.

Spiritually speaking, the old surgical residency rules aren't so crazy after all.

1. Eat when you can.
2. Sleep when you can.

Okay, you can forget rule number 3. The part about the pancreas just doesn't make a good spiritual metaphor.

For Further Reflection

1. Why is rest important—physically and spiritually? Do you get too little or too much rest? What adjustments do you need to make?

2. Have you found Jesus' words about finding rest in him and his burden being light true? Why or why not? How does this play out in your life practically?

3. In what ways does the Spirit urge you to rest, and through what means? How do you generally respond to these urgings? With what results?

4. "Spiritual insomnia occurs when busyness for God takes the place of God's business." Do you agree or disagree? Explain.

5. Which do you value most—relationships or accomplishments? Why? With what consequences?

Chapter Seven

"CAN I HAVE A DRINK OF WATER?"

It's the classic stall tactic for children trying to avoid bedtime. "I want a drink."

The parent sighs. How can you deny the little runt a drink of water? Sure, it might be a stall, but it's a good one. We all know the power of thirst to make everything else of secondary importance.

Think about a time when you were really thirsty. Your mouth was cotton-dry. You were out working in the sun. Dripping sweat. As your body dehydrated, your sodium level in your bloodstream rose as a result of the blood becoming more concentrated. Special receptors near the base of your brain immediately detected the change and began to send out a constant signal: Drink. Drink. Drink![1]

Interestingly, an electrical stimulation of this portion of the brain will result in continuous drinking behavior.[2] (Don't ask me exactly how they figured this out; believe me, you don't really want to know.)

Since our bodies are mostly fluid, have you ever wondered exactly how a proper balance is maintained? After all, serious illness can result from too little or too much fluid. Too little: kidney failure and death. Too much: heart failure and death.

You get the picture. Water balance is important stuff. And God designed the sensation of thirst to urge us to drink to maintain the proper balance. In fact, experiments confirm that animals will consume precisely the needed quantity to keep the concentration of electrolytes in the blood constant.[3]

It's all regulated in the brain by tiny chemoreceptors that send the message, "Drink" or "No need to drink." But it takes time to obey the command. We have to find water, drink it, absorb it into the bloodstream, and let it circulate up to the little receptors in the brain again. Why don't we over-drink in the process?

Because God put several other shut-off mechanisms in place. Number 1: when your mouth is dry, it sends a message of thirst. Immediately. Wetting the mouth with liquid helps shut off this portion of the thirst signal. The next shut-off signal comes from distending the stomach. Experiments have confirmed that filling a balloon that has been placed inside the stomach will result in a cessation of the sensation of thirst.[4] (Again, if you find yourself wincing just thinking about how they did that experiment, it's probably best not to ask. Most likely, the researchers offered a group of medical students deep in educational debt a few hundred dollars. Hungry med students will do almost anything for a buck. For fifty dollars, I let a plastic surgery researcher implant a little capsule under the skin of my left upper arm just to study tissue growth, but that's another story for another time.)

What I really want to talk about is thirst, the thirst that happens naturally as a consequence of how we're designed.

Because without water we're dead.

So thirst is a life-or-death basic.

In Chapter Four, I looked at the metaphor of the body of Christ and suggested that the way water is shared among individual cells in crisis mimics the sharing of the love of God. Every cell is involved in helping maintain blood pressure and water and electrolyte balance.

In review, a physical body needs adequate nutrition in the form of physical food. The body of Christ needs regular balanced intake of the Word of God.

A physical body needs adequate sleep for restoration. The body of Christ needs adequate downtime for refreshing and reflection.

That brings me to the third basic need of the human body—hydration. Water, in liberal quantities, is needed to maintain health and vitality. Considering that water is present in every cell, that it is needed in virtually every metabolic process, and that it makes up a majority of the life-delivering blood, I can offer no spiritual parallel other than love itself.

The need for the body of Christ to stay thoroughly hydrated with the love of God is no less urgent than the daily need of the human body for H_2O. "God is love" (1 John 4:8), and he is to be the context in which every aspect of our life flows. Over and over in the Bible we see the metaphor of God satisfying the thirst of our souls.

> As a deer pants for flowing streams, so pants my soul for you, O God. My soul thirsts for God, for the living God. When shall I come and appear before God?
>
> —Psalm 42:1–2

> O God, you are my God; earnestly I seek you; my
> soul thirsts for you; my flesh faints for you, as in a
> dry and weary land where there is no water. So I
> have looked upon you in the sanctuary, beholding
> your power and glory. Because your *steadfast love*
> is better than life, my lips will praise you.
>> —Psalm 63:1–3, *emphasis mine*

Intimacy like David experienced with the Father is so precious. And the closer we draw to the heart of the Father, the more we experience new facets of his love, to the point that we understand his love as better than life itself.

The Cure for Soul Dehydration

All of us have experienced soul thirst like this. Perhaps you are experiencing dehydration of soul, and that's why you picked up this book. You've been plodding along, going through the motions, your prayers seeming to bounce off an empty heaven. Take courage. Even a man after God's heart, David, experienced soul dehydration. Come to your Heavenly Father and drink. Pull away to lay your head upon his chest. Nestle in to hear his heartbeat. There is only one fountain that can satisfy.

> I stretch out my hands to you; my soul thirsts for you
> like a parched land. Answer me quickly, O Lord!
> My spirit fails! Hide not your face from me, lest I be
> like those who go down to the pit. Let me hear in the
> morning of your *steadfast love*, for in you I trust.
>> —Psalm 143:6–8a, *emphasis mine*

It isn't an accident that David's references to God's love fall right on the tails of his expression of thirst. Look at his use of simile in two of the passages above. "As in a dry and weary land" and "like a parched land." I've been there. Dry. Crusty. No fruit.

I remember a time of spiritual dryness I experienced while a freshman in college. I was off at Eastern Mennonite College (now University) and was spending a whole lot more time with my chemistry textbook and other studies than I was with the Word of God. I was focused on a goal: medical school acceptance. Nothing else seemed to matter much in those days. I studied most waking hours. And my soul suffered.

As school was winding up close to the Christmas holidays, the format for required chapel services was adjusted. The chapel auditorium was open for private prayer and meditation while one of the professors played soft background organ music. I'd been away from home for two years at that point, having attended my last year of high school boarding on the same campus. I was becoming a man, and I was aware that somewhere in the midst of growing up I'd pushed aside my ability to cry. I remember thinking about it. I just couldn't cry. It was as if in my attempt at manliness, I'd just shoved that display of emotion aside, and I thought I'd moved beyond it.

Until God's love broke in during a silent chapel service.

I opened my leather Bible to the book of Hosea and began to read.

> When Israel was a child, I loved him, and out of Egypt I called my son. The more they were called, the more they went away; they kept sacrificing to the Baals and burning offerings to idols. Yet it was I who taught Ephraim to walk; I took them up by their arms, but they did not know that I healed them.
>
> —11:1–3

I began to understand God's voice speaking to me across the ages through an Old Testament prophet. *God loves me! He is acting on my behalf, drawing me, calling me, even when I go my own way!* I continued reading.

> I led them with cords of kindness, with the bands
> of love. . . .
>
> —11:4a

When he leads me, it may feel like restriction, cords, or bands, but it is really his love. I read down the page until my eyes fixed on verse 8.

> How can I give you up, O Ephraim? How can I hand
> you over, O Israel?

My eyes began to tear up. I kept thinking about a movie they had shown earlier that year, *The Other Side of the Mountain*. It was based on the life of Jill Kinmont, a snow skier, an Olympic hopeful for 1956 who was paralyzed in a skiing accident. A scene kept replaying in my mind, in which Jill's boyfriend, played by Beau Bridges, was standing on the side of the road pleading with her to accept his love. Jill, now living out her life in a wheelchair, had pushed him away, thinking herself unworthy. The scene is a dramatic one, with Bridges crying and basically saying that he can't see how he could go on without her.

How can I give you up? I asked God silently. *I am the disabled one. God is whole. Yet he says this to me.*

His love is there, behind every circumstance of our lives, holding us, drawing us, sustaining us.

During our faithfulness. And during our faithlessness.

Remember Hosea's story? God led him to love and marry a prostitute, a woman who would commit adultery with other lovers, just to serve as a picture of Israel whoring after other gods. Later God speaks through Hosea to us, a message of his love even when we were unaware that his goodness was being extended. A message that was not only written but demonstrated in the life of the prophet.

Remember what I said about love being a real get-your-hands-dirty concept? Hosea shows us how it's done.

Now we are the ones receiving the tender love of God. We are the disabled. Unworthy. Constantly turning away from the fountain of living waters to refresh our souls with indiscretion. Yet God is here, gently nudging us with love with every pulse of his heart.

He is the perfect one, strong and faithful, in need of nothing to complete himself, yet allowing his own heart to break over our refusal to be loved. And over our escapades with other lovers.

Thirsty? Come!

He created the body of Christ to require a constant supply of his love. He created us to thirst! And he holds out the invitation to all who feel parchedness of soul.

> Come, everyone who thirsts, come to the waters; and
> he who has no money, come, buy and eat! Come, buy
> wine and milk without money and without price.
>
> —Isaiah 55:1

I love the interaction between Jesus and the Samaritan woman at the well. He captures the soul thirst issue in a poignant setting.

> "Everyone who drinks of this water will be thirsty
> again, but whoever drinks of the water that I will

give him will never be thirsty again. The water that
I will give him will become in him a spring of water
welling up to eternal life."

—John 4:13–14

What a beautiful picture of how a life lived in the fullness of
God's love spills over to others, the evidence of the heart-change
that springs out of salvation.

After completion of an intestinal surgery, say, a resection of a
portion of the large intestine for cancer, I sit down to write the
nursing instructions. Because I've physically handled the bowel,
I know the patient won't be ready to take fluids by mouth for
a few days, but I know the patient has hourly requirements for
fluid. Since the patient can't drink, what will I do?

We still give the patient fluid, but it is given directly into
the bloodstream in the form of an intravenous drip through a
small tube inserted into a vein. For normal-sized adults, I give
one hundred cc's of fluid each hour for maintenance needs and
additional fluid based on an estimation of the patient's other
fluid losses during or after surgery. If I'm concerned, I'll be
sure the patient has a urinary catheter so I can monitor exactly
how much fluid the patient urinates away. If the patient's urine
volume goes down, it's often a sign that he or she isn't getting
enough fluid in.

You see, God designed us in a fascinating way, with hundreds
of feedback systems designed to maintain balance. As soon as
the brain senses that there isn't enough fluid around (dehydration), a special hormone called ADH (antidiuretic hormone)
is sent as a messenger to the kidneys: "Preserve fluid! Don't
share. Don't give off water."

Likewise, one of the first things that happens to the soul that
isn't saturated in God's love is a shutdown of the overflow of
that love into the world. The solution is obvious.

Drink in his love. Sip, gulp, and slurp without worrying if anyone is watching. Let it drip from your chin. Forget your table manners. Knock back a pint of 100 proof love of God.

Drink it in.

Then share it with Kevin.

For Further Reflection

1. What does it mean to you to thirst for God? Do you thirst for his presence and love like a parched wanderer in the desert? If not, why not?

2. Do you ever feel like your prayers are bouncing off heaven? Why? What can you do to feel closer to God and to feel his closeness to you?

3. Why did God tell his prophet Hosea to marry a prostitute? Has God ever done anything that radical to remind you of his love? How did you respond?

4. Do you agree that "God created the body of Christ to require a constant supply of his love? He created us to thirst"? How does this work out in your life?

5. Is God's love flowing through you? If not, why not? How can you allow a greater stream of divine affection into your heart and life?

Chapter Eight

BREATHING GRACE

I'd never intentionally hold your head underwater.

Unless I was desperate for air and trying to save myself. Then all bets are off. When we are dying, instinct kicks in, and we struggle for oxygen even at the expense of pulling down the others around us.

I remember a game we played back at Highland Retreat Camp the summer after my love affair with Paul McCartney's cute blonde cousin.

It was a great recipe for fun. Or disaster. Take twenty fifth- and sixth-grade boys and one greased watermelon. Put them both in a swimming pool. Mix thoroughly with physical competition, and sprinkle with laughter. Serve and enjoy.

The boys were divided into teams. A slippery watermelon was thrown into the middle of the pool. The goal was to guide, push, heave, or otherwise manipulate the fruit to the side of the pool opposite your starting side. While everyone on the other side tried to push the melon onto your side, of course. That's pretty much it. I don't remember any other rules.

I do remember the tangle of arms and bodies all struggling to keep our heads above water, noses and mouths open to the supply of air as we fought the opposition in our attempt to push the melon across the deep end.

I remember the stark fear in the face of one of my friends who broke the surface of the water gasping and accusing us of depriving him of air.

Going a few seconds without oxygen brings our priorities into perspective. Nothing else matters. It's breathe or die. Now.

Without eating, we'll die in weeks to months. Without drinking, we'll succumb to the grim reaper in days. Without oxygen, we have only minutes. And within seconds, our brain is sending out a constant, pressing imperative: Breathe! Breathe! *BREATHE!*

So it is with the body of Christ. To expect the body to thrive, to behave as our spiritual DNA has mandated, certain items are needed in constant supply. We've talked about the balanced nutrition of the Word of God, the need for rest, and drinking deeply of his love. Now I want to talk to you about the life-giving gospel of grace.

Grace?

Absolutely.

Our need to find our way constantly saturated with the gospel of grace is no less critical to the spiritual vitality of the body of Christ than is our physical need for oxygen. Most of us have heard that we are saved by grace. But do we really need it every moment, like oxygen? I can imagine your objections. Perhaps they are based on a limited understanding about what grace really is.

Our culture has softened its meaning. Grace is a quality of refinement. Like being genteel. Or we think it's just being kind.

It can be those things. But it's much richer.

Or we think of God's grace being extended to us only when something good happens. *That car missed us by inches! That was grace!*

True. But I assure you, if the car wouldn't have missed, *that would have been God's grace as well.*

Perhaps your definition of grace needs to be expanded. As I have put it elsewhere:

Grace is a godly characteristic that determines God's posture toward his children whereby he generously and freely loves, forgives, favors, and exalts undeserving sinners into sonship.[1]

Just as we were saved by grace, we are to continue in grace, and everything we do is enabled by God's grace.

> But grow in the grace and knowledge of our Lord and Savior Jesus Christ.
>
> —2 Peter 3:18

> As each has received a gift, use it to serve one another, as good stewards of God's varied grace: whoever speaks, as one who speaks oracles of God; whoever serves, as one who serves by the strength that God supplies—in order that in everything God may be glorified through Jesus Christ. To him belong glory and dominion forever and ever. Amen.
>
> —1 Peter 4:10–11

Walking in the truth of the gospel of grace means I have given up the false gospels I was clinging to in order to become more acceptable to God. The gospel of grace recognizes that the sacrifice of Christ on the cross is completely sufficient to place me in right standing with my Heavenly Father. Anything else I do to excuse my poor behavior or to make myself more acceptable to God is reliance on a false gospel. The only true gospel says the cross is enough. I love the way the J. B. Phillips paraphrase reads:

> Christ means the end of the struggle for righteousness.
>
> —Romans 10:4

When I am walking in my false gospel of pride, I am saying, "I'm not really that bad" or "I'm not as bad as the next guy."

When I'm walking in a false gospel of works, I say in effect, "I'll be more acceptable if I perform well. God will love me more if only . . ."

But I fall in and out of a proper understanding of the gospel of grace almost as easily as I breathe. I have to fight the self-deception of impure motives with liberal and frequent reminders of God's grace to me.

God's grace to me is a constant. It is the assurance that his love for me will always be the same, *regardless of my behavior, independent of my "worth."*

Love expressed only when I perform well is wages.

Love expressed when I'm behaving like a scoundrel is grace.

And that becomes the foundation for transforming my heart to beat like his. I can begin to love others in spite of their behavior only when I understand that I am loved "just as I am, without one plea."

The gospel of grace means I "get to."

If God loved me only when I deserve it, that would result in behavior modification. Being a skin-Christian. That is, only looking like a Christian on the outside.

God's loving me even though I'm undeserving results in heart transformation.

In that condition, walking in a saturation of grace, I can find the only real avenue to serve others with right motives. Service without a hitch. A free lunch. No small writing at the bottom of the page. No legal loopholes. Just service for benevolence's sake, the essence of love.

At the top of a page in my Bible I've written, "The only way to love is through the freedom of the gospel." Likely that quote is something I heard from Phil Smuland, my pastor at the time. It may be original with him or may have sprung from something I read. Regardless of the source, I believe it's absolutely true. The only way I can begin to participate in the essence of being Christian—that is, loving others—is through the freedom that comes through the gospel of grace. Love becomes a "get to." The "have to's" have been left on the curbside hoping to be picked up by a false-gospel adherent. As we turn away from the need to be good enough to accept the righteousness that is ours because of the cross, "Have-to" will be left commiserating on the bench with "Should've" and "Could've," while we are free to play the game of loving the fellow members of the body of Christ.

> For you were called to freedom, brothers. Only do not use your freedom as an opportunity for the flesh, but through love serve one another. For the whole law is fulfilled in one word: "You shall love your neighbor as yourself."
>
> —Galatians 5:13–14

> Now the Lord is the Spirit, and where the Spirit of the Lord is, there is freedom.
>
> —2 Corinthians 3:17

The gospel of grace finds its expression in love. If you operate out of a works-gospel, duty rather than devotion will take center stage. Paul says it this way:

> For in Christ Jesus neither circumcision nor uncircumcision counts for anything, but only *faith working through love.*
>
> —Galatians 5:6, *emphasis mine*

That's the real bottom line for love, isn't it? Love finds its purest expression in the tenderness of the gospel. We are accepted and loved because of the work of the cross, Jesus Christ's death in our place, bearing the punishment for our sins, an act of pure grace. That wasn't anything we deserved. It became ours by faith alone. We saw earlier in 1 Corinthians 13 that any wonderful deed falls flat without love, and here we see that "neither circumcision" (working to be accepted), "nor uncircumcision" (going my way) amounts to anything of value. True value is found only in love as an expression of the gospel of grace.

I'm a missionary because of grace. I get to love. As a part of the body of Christ, I get to soothe the wounds of the suffering. I get to be his hands. With love as our motivation, it's all "get to." Let "have to" and "should've" rot on the garbage heap with the devil who originated the deception of needing to make ourselves acceptable to God.

When my second son, Evan, was three years old, he participated in a small Christmas play put on by the children in our congregation back in Mt. Crawford, Virginia. He was an extra, a part of the angelic host. A supporting role. You parents know what I'm talking about. If you don't get to be Mary or Joseph, a shepherd, or at least a wise man, you get relegated to the angelic host or, even worse, made to crawl around with some sheep wool on your back as a part of the animal supporting cast.

But Evan didn't see his role as lesser or inferior. Not at all. As the children acted out the manger scene, instead of staying off to the side, stage left, Evan quickly manipulated his way front and center right behind baby Jesus. There he happily observed the inner sanctum of the blessed family. That was so typical of his self-confidence. Why shouldn't he be in the center? He had the cool angel outfit complete with cardboard wings, didn't he? He couldn't have imagined that his place should be anywhere but right in the middle of the action with Joseph, Mary, and Jesus himself.

But as the play continued, Evan moved to the very front of the stage, facing the audience to make a proclamation. Of course, knowing that our son did not have a speaking part, my wife and I wondered just what our little son had in mind! Evan raised his voice loud enough for us to hear near the back of the building. "I just want my mom!"

With that, he launched himself off the stage and ran down the aisle to plop his angelic backside on his mother's lap!

Evan went from center-stage confident to needing his mommy at warp speed.

Silly? Not for a three-year-old.

And not so different from me as I'm learning to walk in the gospel of grace. One moment I'm aware of God's presence. I'm front and center with Jesus, confident of the work he has done on my behalf. A minute later, I'm needin'-my-mommy insecure, critical of my brother, operating out of a false gospel of pride.

Oh, how effortlessly I move from one to the other. Not that it's a supply problem. Grace is abundant. The problem is my recognition.

The nearly seamless way I move from grace to self-reliance (or self-condemnation, also a symptom of hidden pride) is the very reason I need grace awareness in a constant supply.

Like oxygen.

Every second.

Grace respiration. Relying on the sufficiency of the cross every moment.

The spiritual life of the body of Christ depends on it.

Twenty-five Trillion Specialized Oxygen Deliverers

The human body contains 100 trillion individual cells, specialized little units all relying on a constant supply of oxygen. Fortunately, a remarkable network of blood vessels are arranged in millions of capillaries, so that the oxygen from the blood is available to each cell. Amazingly, of the 100 trillion cells, twenty-five trillion of them are red blood cells, the blood cells that carry hemoglobin molecules specializing in transporting oxygen. My point? Just that one out of every four cells in the body is specially designed to deliver oxygen. The sheer number of cells needed for the constant job of oxygen transportation speaks of the relative importance of their function.

As important as the red cells delivering oxygen are the multiple grace-deliverers bringing us spiritual health. Prayer. Fellowship with other believers. The Word. All are part of the needed army of grace-transporters necessary for our survival and effectiveness.

Without oxygen every moment, our metabolic processes quickly unravel into inefficiency. In several minutes unconsciousness ensues. And death follows quickly on the heels of unconsciousness. Without oxygen, cells can never do the job they've been called to do.

The physical body depends on it.

And I need to walk in the awareness of grace every hour, every minute.

The health of the body of Christ depends on it.

Because without it, we'll never live out our calling:

Love. Love. Love!

For Further Reflection

1. Do you feel the continual need of grace as strongly as you feel the need for oxygen? Why or why not?

2. Do you agree that God is showing us his grace as much when tragedy occurs as when everything goes smoothly? How could God's allowing a severe trial be a sign of his kindness toward us?

3. What does walking in the true grace of God have to do with renouncing false gospels? What are some of these false gospels?

4. Do you agree that God's love for you will always be the same, regardless of your behavior, independent of your "worth"?

5. Can you identify with the author's comments, "One moment I'm aware of God's presence. I'm front and center with Jesus, confident of the work he has done on my behalf. A minute later, I'm needin'-my-mommy insecure, critical of my brother, operating out of a false gospel of pride"? Is it evidence of weakness or strength that we feel we need God the way a youngster needs his mother?

Part Three

Prescriptions
for Failing Hearts

Chapter Nine

FAILURE TO THRIVE

I t is easy for a single mother in Africa to lose hope.

Mary Wambui nestled her two-year-old child to her breast to soothe his whimpering during the bumpy ride down to Kijabe Hospital. The child, her first and only, had been losing weight. The previous night he awoke in a pool of sweat, and she'd had to change his diaper four times because of his diarrhea.

Mary stroked his face, noting how the skin stretched tight across his bones. *Why does Daniel stay so sick? He's had lung infections twice in the last year. I'm trying to feed him ugali and rice, but he just doesn't seem to grow.*

She carried him into the clinic and watched as a nurse took his vital signs and measured his weight.

The nurse ran her finger over a weight chart. *Only nine and a half kilograms.* "How old is he?"

"Twenty-five months." Mary tried to stay calm, but she didn't like the way the nurse frowned when she looked at her son.

"I'll call the doctor."

In picking up this patient's chart, looking only at the brief recorded nursing history and the weight, a physician is able to make a breadbasket diagnosis: failure to thrive. I use the term *breadbasket* because it's a catch-all diagnosis. Literally hundreds of things can cause a child to topple and fall off the growth charts. With a relatively simple equation to calculate what the weight is supposed to be, the physician knows that his patient is failing to thrive. Then the Sherlock Holmes business begins. Why is the patient losing weight?

Gastroesophageal reflux, lactose intolerance, pancreatic insufficiency, inflammatory bowel disease, cystic fibrosis, hypothyroidism, diabetes mellitus, parasitic infections, tuberculosis, lead poisoning, cancer, or hundreds of other things could be the underlying cause. So with limited resources, what is the physician in Africa to do?

There are some simple rules in medicine to help keep the sleepy physician on track. One is: common things are common.

In Africa, that means AIDS.

So they did an HIV antibody test. And they found the underlying cause. The baby had AIDS.

AIDS in a child? I thought that was the result of sharing needles to do intravenous drugs or of sleeping around. How does an innocent child contract HIV?

Yes, HIV occurs in children in Africa. It's called maternal child transmission, and the virus is passed to the innocent during the birth process or after birth during breastfeeding. Ironic, huh? The child contracts an illness doing what he was designed to do—hunger and drink.

HIV attacks the body's ability to resist infection, devastating the population of white blood cells designed to fight invasion. When a host's defense is decimated, infections have free rein. For this child, having HIV paved the way to developing pulmonary tuberculosis and caused susceptibility to a gastrointestinal infection that kept him from utilizing the calories he took in.

Equally tragic, a failure to thrive is also seen within the body of Christ and can begin, like HIV, with the infection of individual cells. Is the body of Christ falling off the chart of expected growth?

Is a weakening of our spiritual immune system robbing us of our ability to love?

Just as HIV hampers the ability of the body to recognize and fight foreign invaders, so a weak spiritual immune system keeps us from recognizing and countering the deception of false gospels. Okay, I've used the term *false gospel* before. It's time to define it.

A false gospel is anything I attempt to make myself acceptable to God *outside of the cross, outside of or in addition to Christ's death for me as the only way to God.* I operate out of the false gospel of pride anytime I excuse my sinfulness. *I'm not as bad as the next guy. At least I don't* _____. I'm operating out of the false gospel of works anytime I think God will like me better because I've performed well.

Rely on anything outside of Christ for right standing with the Father, and you're standing on a false gospel.

The good news of the gospel is that Jesus Christ's death on a cruel cross is completely sufficient to place me in right standing before a perfect, holy God. Every good thing I do, every act of love poured into the lives of others, every kind word spoken and every dime given is a get-to, a want-to when I am operating from within the framework of the true gospel.

When the same actions are carried out in a "have-to" works-gospel, the result is a big zero.

> If I give away all I have, and if I deliver up my body
> to be burned, but have not love, I gain nothing.
>   —1 Corinthians 13:3

The true gospel is the good news that states:

> But God, being rich in mercy, because of the great
> love with which he loved us, even when we were
> dead in our trespasses, made us alive together with
> Christ—by grace you have been saved. . . . For by
> grace you have been saved through faith. And this
> is not your own doing; it is the gift of God, not a
> result of works, so that no one may boast.
>   —Ephesians 2:4–5, 8–9

I'm saved not as a result of being good but as a result of Christ's goodness that has been applied to my account. That's the gospel of grace.

We fail to recognize the false-gospel foreign invader when our spiritual immune system is malfunctioning.

What are the primary false gospels that we succumb to when our spiritual immune system is not up and running? I believe there are many, but two stand out at the front of a long line of enemies.

The first is *legalism*—that is, the idea that anything I do makes me a bit more acceptable to God. Legalism or a works-gospel is at the very heart of a major evangelical world religion, Islam. A faithful Muslim can never be quite sure whether the scales of good deeds are tipped in his favor, outweighing the bad. Reaching paradise under such a system favors a flurry of outward behaviors, exact rules to follow for washings, postures for prayers, and the correct memorization of words.

The works-gospel at the core of Islam isn't confined to religions outside of Christianity. But within the Christian church, legalism hides behind a cloak of good deeds, with only God himself seeing the motive of the heart.

The horror of it to me is that I can slip into the attitudes of legalism if I'm not constantly vigilant. One moment I'm resting in the confidence of God's forgiveness. The next, I'm beating myself up for some long-forgotten offense. Guilt feelings, the way we chastise ourselves for past sins, seem to be a favorite weapon of our enemy to pull us off track and tempt us with falling into a works-gospel.

How does this work? Let's look at the downward spiral so typical for us when we listen to the whispers of Satan or when our own minds convince us of our unworthiness.

I blew it again. Lust. Unkind words. The self-righteous way I correct my children when I've fallen in the same way a thousand times. We wallow in gut-tightening anxiety because we fear that God is displeased with us. Again. I'm not saying we shouldn't acknowledge our sin. That's the essence of repentance to bring us back into fellowship with God. What I'm suggesting is that the rumination, the dwelling in mental defeat that follows, compounds the sin. We feel that a certain amount of groveling or bad feelings should be endured for a time to pay for the wrong that we've done. The buzzer sounds—*Wrong!* Yes, sin brings remorse, and that sorrow leads us to repentance, but we need to leave it at that point and focus on the truth of the gospel. My sin was paid for on Calvary. Jesus' record is now mine. No amount of time spent crawling around in my own condemnation will change that or make me more acceptable to God.

The works-gospel is deceptive because it wears a cloak of good deeds. We like to serve soup at the homeless shelter, but we park our car in front so everyone will see we're there.

Do we like to bring up praise reports that highlight not God but the fact that he chose to use us? The difference is subtle and therefore scary.

We bring up prayer requests not because we really want prayer, but because we want to emphasize someone else's sin. *I'm not as bad as the next guy!*

We want to give anonymously, but we're glad that at least the church treasurer and our accountant will know of our gift.

Have you ever been upset at the behavior of your child in public? Was that because it reflected badly on you or your parenting skills? That's operating out of the false gospel of pride, a form of the works-gospel. *I need to be seen to be good.*

Have you ever felt unworthy of Christ's love? Who hasn't?

When we find ourselves riding down the slope of self-depreciation, we're riding in a car emblazoned with a sponsor's logo.

Self-deception is subtle and by nature isn't recognizable to the one being deceived. That frightens me. Sometimes only my spouse can see when my motives are tainted. At those times, my natural reaction is to defend myself rather than to humbly take off the pride-blinders that have given me such tunnel vision about an issue.

The second false gospel standing in line to deceive is what some have dubbed *the prosperity gospel*. In essence, it works like this. I work—God rewards. I give not because of get-to but because a carrot of reward is dangled in front of me. My comfort becomes God (rather than God being my comfort), the idol that I serve. Blessings become the point of my focus, over and above the one who blesses. Gifts, not the giver, receive the glory.

This prosperity gospel can also be subtle. Overspending on self in the name of God's financial blessings is a temptation that many U.S. Christians face. Author and teacher Randy Alcorn cuts straight to the wallet when he states that God blesses us financially "not to raise my standard of living but to raise my standard of giving."[1]

This is another area where I have to watch my tendency to engage in self-deceit. *I need the new furniture so I can invite over my colleagues and share the gospel with them. I need a new game room so the teens can come over to our house.* All of those things may be true, but sometimes the distance between self-serving and Christ-serving is razor-thin.

Sometimes the distance between self-serving and Christ-serving can be as thin as a new flat-screen TV.

Wealthy Christian, hear me out before you toss this book aside! Are possessions wrong? No. Can they tempt our heart away from the fountain of living water? Yes. Are material possessions blessings from God? Yes. If we give everything away, but not out of love, is it worth anything? No!

The difference is in *our attitudes* about possessions and wealth. Every good thing should be received as a gift from God and should be held with an open hand, recognizing that God's abundance to us is a blessing meant to help us with our primary task as members of the body of Christ: loving God and loving our neighbors.

It is the job of the immune system to identify foreign invaders, the pathologic viruses and bacteria that sicken us and weaken our ability to function the way we are designed. To do this properly, lymphocytes (a type of white blood cell, defenders of our wellness) have to attend a school of sorts, learning what to attack as foreign and what to accept as "me." Once school is done, the immune system retains a state of *constant vigilance* to keep us well.

It's the same in the body of Christ. We need to pay attention to the basics (as we've already discussed—food, water, sleep, oxygen) in order to stay healthy. We need to continue our study of God's Word, daily reminding our souls of the truth of the gospel of grace. That way when a counterfeit or a foreign invader comes along, we're ready.

Don't forget the war metaphors used frequently in the New Testament.

> Finally, be strong in the Lord and in the strength of his might. Put on the whole armor of God, that you may be able to stand against the schemes of the devil. For we do not wrestle against flesh and blood, but against the rulers, against the authorities, against the cosmic powers over this present darkness, against the spiritual forces of evil in the heavenly places. Therefore take up the whole armor of God, that you may be able to withstand in the evil day, and having done all, to stand firm. Stand therefore, having fastened on the belt of truth, and having put on the breastplate of righteousness, and, as shoes for your feet, having put on the readiness given by the gospel of peace. In all circumstances take up the shield of faith, with which you can extinguish all the flaming darts of the evil one; and take the helmet of salvation, and the sword of the Spirit, which is the word of God.
>
> —Ephesians 6:10–17

While writing this chapter, I took an exercise break and walked out through the forests around Kijabe, Kenya. I've been on these trails dozens of times and enjoy observing the dik-diks, baboons, Colobus monkeys, and other wildlife. I noticed something today. The one path up from Kijabetown to the hospital, traveled by many hospital employees, was well-worn—a bit rocky in places, but without any overgrowth. When I moved off the dusty road toward the railroad track, the path changed. Grass grew tall, and bushes reached in from both sides to narrow the trail.

Why? Because the pathway to the railroad track is lightly traveled, so troublesome overgrowth isn't trampled down.

It made me think about the necessity of traveling through the Scriptures concerning the gospel of grace over and over to keep down the growth of cares and other take-advantage weeds that occur when I'm not traveling the path often enough. Traveling well-worn Scripture pathways to keep down soul-overgrowth is akin to the vigilance that is needed in our defense against false gospels.

It's a human tendency to slide into thought patterns that spiral downward, away from the wonderful truth that we are loved, that we are God's beloved, the princess that he rescued from the evil one to be his bride. What a sad tragedy—how forgetful we are of the tenderness with which he graces our lives. Over and over again we turn from the fountain not suddenly but gradually, believing first a whisper of our unworthiness, then a lie about his love. Soon we are mud-covered and wallowing in the sewer of our false gospels while the fountain of his grace flows free but shielded from our hearts by an umbrella of unbelief in our position as his lover.

The process, this slippery thought-slide from rejoicing in the fountain to self-deprecation, needs to be recognized and rejected. Paul speaks of powerful spiritual weapons that can combat every errant thought.

> For though we walk in the flesh, we are not waging
> war according to the flesh. For the weapons of our
> warfare are not of the flesh but have divine power
> to destroy strongholds. We destroy arguments and
> every lofty opinion raised against the knowledge of
> God, and take every thought captive to obey Christ,
> being ready to punish every disobedience, when your
> obedience is complete.
>
> —2 Corinthians 10:3–6

What happened to Mary Wambui's child? He was admitted to Kijabe Hospital, rehydrated, placed on a high-protein, liquid food supplement, and started on antibiotics to fight his tuberculosis. In other words, other than the antibiotics, everything that was done was *attention to the basics: water, food, rest, and oxygen.*

Spiritual immune incompetence (the inability to fight off disease and remain healthy) is treated the same way.

There is no fast, magic-bullet treatment to fix a failure to thrive. While helping the church where it is falling off the growth charts is a huge problem, it is one that can be overcome. In addition to a disciplined approach to the basic health needs of the body of Christ, we need to apply constant vigilance to recognize and refute the challenges of the false gospels.

The reputation of Christ in this world depends on it.

For Further Reflection

1. Have you observed a failure to thrive in the body of Christ, whether in yourself or others? What causes this?

2. Did your own goodness have anything to do with God's bringing you into his family? Does it have anything to

do with his continuing to love you? Support your answer with Scripture.

3. How would you define *legalism*? What makes legalism unhealthy or even dangerous? How can you detect this enemy in your own life? How can you guard against it or become free of it?

4. Is the prosperity gospel really a false gospel? Doesn't God promise us rewards if we serve him? How is that promise distorted or misunderstood in the prosperity gospel?

5. What thought patterns or spiritual misunderstandings are keeping you from basking in God's love or are leading you to wallow in dirty streams or self-reliance? What will you do about this?

Chapter Ten

THE C-WORD

I love the sunshine. Warmth on my skin on a cool afternoon. Long summer evenings back in Virginia, when light stretched all the way 'til nine o'clock. There's nothing like the sun to nudge a dragging soul toward a smile.

I love watching the sunset from my veranda. The monochromatic sky splits into a hundred hues of orange, filtering through the dust over the African Rift Valley. I like sunrise even more, though I rarely see it, unless I escape to the Indian Ocean for a vacation. The horizon begins to color, announcing the arrival of the sun, and soon we're all looking for a respite from the blistering heat. The pace slows, and the tourists park themselves within striking range of the pool, like animals gathering around a waterhole in Maasai Mara.

But the sun is death for a young Somali boy I operated on this week. He came to Kijabe from a refugee camp. Underweight, malnourished, and blind, his skin was dry and aged beyond his years. He has a rare condition known as xeroderma pigmentosa, an inherited abnormality because of which his skin is unable to repair damage from the sun's rays.

Walk outside under the bright sun for a few moments. The sun's invisible rays pass through our skin unseen and mostly undetected. Thanks to a huge educational effort, most of us know of the damaging effects of the sun's radiation. Responsible parents slather their children with sunscreen before trips to the local pool. It's a laudable effort that will prevent the occurrence of life-threatening skin cancers down the line.

Our DNA is the chief recipient of the rays' bombardment, suffering the severing of molecular bonds at the mercy of the sun. And for the most part our cells contain the molecular machinery to fight back, to rebuild any damage experienced in our moment-by-moment interaction with radiation.

But not so in the case of a patient with xeroderma pigmentosa. For XP patients, the sun is lethal. They can't be allowed to experience any sunlight, as they are unable to repair the damaging effects of sunlight radiation. Imagine a life where you weren't allowed to sit next to a window, a life where the smell of Coppertone didn't remind you of a lovely beach vacation but served as a daily reminder of your mortality. Imagine a life in which you weren't allowed outdoors, a life in which even the reflected rays of a full moon could be enough to send your cell's machinery toward a path of premature aging and transformation into cancer.

My patient, a frail boy of seven years, already had patchy areas of sun damage all across his face and a large, oozing pink cancer mushrooming off his lower lip. Look at him quickly as you pass his hospital room, and you might think that his tongue is protruding. A little boy just being seven. But look closer, and the realization will hit: *that's not his tongue!*

Cancer. It's just not what you expect to happen to seven-year-old boys.

Cancer.

Just the word prods anxiety to grip us in burning stomach upset. Cancer. It can be fatal. Not always so, but often prompting us to ride a train of fear with the unknown as a cruel conductor. At home I'd often find myself in conversation with a patient, needing to tell him or her that I'd made a diagnosis of cancer, but wanting to ease into the reality of the concept, so he or she would be able to absorb what I was saying. It's often best to approach slowly, using words like *growth* or *mass* or even *tumor* before using the dreaded c-word. If you say cancer first and then go on to explain treatment options, the whole conversation may be lost to the patient, who has heard little since the word *cancer* spilled from the surgeon's lips.

Some of us have lost loved ones to cancer. Others have battled it themselves. And some, though they've heard the word a thousand times, are still a bit mystified as to just what it is.

In essence, cancer is a growth of tissue, rebellious and selfish in attitude, that stops obeying the unwritten ground rules of behavior. The cells of cancer live only for themselves, become disrespectful of others' boundaries, and often spread to other parts of the body by blood or tissue channels, leaving their offspring to grow at the expense of the normal cells around them. Sometimes cancer grows rapidly to its own detriment, outgrowing even the blood vessels needed to bring in the nutrients this hungry tissue demands. Cancer like this grows rapidly at the edges where the supply lines are intact but rots away in the interior because the cancer cells at the periphery are getting all the nutrition.

Unchecked, cancer's selfish behavior threatens life, stealing all the available energy and nutrition so that it can grow, regardless of whether that growth impinges on a life-giving function.

One of the most disheartening things I see in Africa is cancer neglect. Perhaps that isn't the right word for it exactly, but in effect that's what happens. Cancer goes untreated, growing, having its own way as patients weaken to the point that the chances of cure are minuscule. The reasons for this neglect are manifold. Poverty. Ignorance. The delays are compounded by witch doctors promising a cure but delivering only pain and false hope.

The day I operated on my little xeroderma pigmentosa patient was all too typical. After my young Somali patient's case where I resected most of his lower lip, I faced the challenge of a woman who had allowed a cancer to overtake the majority of her breast. In the West I rarely saw a breast cancer that I could actually feel. A woman would get referred because of an abnormality seen on a routine mammogram, an angry little grouping of calcifications perhaps or a worrisome shadow deep within the normal tissue that wouldn't be palpable for years. But not in Kenya. Here there are no mammography screening programs. Here there are only worrisome lumps felt on exam and, worse yet, often ignored for years until the growth is unsightly, a livid, weeping tumor poking up through skin that has been eaten away or crowded aside.

I examined my breast cancer patient's chest X-ray and quizzed my intern. "What do you see?"

"No lung metastasis."

"Look closer."

The mistake is in looking only at the lungs. The patient's affected breast was noticeably larger and denser because of the infiltration of cancer. We're not accustomed to looking for signs of breast cancer within the breast on a chest X-ray, but my patient's case was so advanced that even a routine chest film was markedly abnormal.

Operating on advanced cases makes for challenging surgery. In the West we've moved to minimal surgeries, relying on post-op radiation and chemotherapy to assist in the fight. In Africa, surgery is often the only available option. To gain local control, I used a technique taught to me by a visiting plastic surgeon from Australia. After removing the breast and most of the surrounding involved skin, I rotated a large flap of muscle and skin from the patient's back around to cover the defect. I wasn't reconstructing the breast, mind you. I was only trying to get good durable coverage of the large defect left after removing the cancer.

After I finished the breast cancer surgery, I was faced with another patient with a different kind of cancer, again long beyond a cure. After months of difficulty in swallowing, my middle-aged male patient sought our help. The problem began with the uncomfortable sensation that meat was hanging up in the chest during eating. But that alone wasn't enough to prompt him to come in. Slowly, month after month, the situation worsened, progressing to difficulty with even getting liquids to pass. The weight loss is usually impressive, and these patients often look as if their skin barely stretches over their skulls.

It was yet another case of esophageal cancer, an epidemic problem in Kenya. Carefully I looked down the esophagus with the assistance of an endoscope, an instrument that allows us to get a view of just what the problem may be. Predictably, I found a bulky cancer blocking the flow of food down the esophagus, the muscular tube that connects the back of the throat with the stomach. Because of the blockage, I probed gently to pass a small guide wire past the cancer. Then larger and larger dilators were passed over the wire to stretch the esophagus open again. Finally, once the esophagus had been opened (essentially splitting apart the occluding cancer), a stent was placed to allow food to pass through the area of cancer.

After such a procedure, the patient is encouraged to sit up and is given the first ceremonial drink of water. The expression of surprise is memorable. *I can swallow again!*

Remember the definition of love we gave back in Chapter Four? We borrowed from Dallas Willard:

> And first, what exactly is love? It is *will to good* or "bene-volence." We love something or someone when we promote its good for its own sake. Love's contrary is malice, and its simple absence is indifference.[1]

Cancer behaves in a way exactly opposite love. Cancer cells do not will good to their neighbors. Cancer cells are all about self. *Me, me, me!* I want my space. My time. My will. My way. "Feed me" is cancer's cry. The cancer philosophy is one of serving self above serving others. It is me first and then see what's left over for my neighbor.

It is this cancer attitude in myself that I must fight with the same diligence that surgeons use to attack cancer. Early, before it is so rooted that the surgery is difficult and painful.

In answering a call to follow Jesus, we find ourselves quickly face to face with the essence of what loving our neighbor is all about. And we're suddenly in trouble. *I've fallen in love with Jesus, and the first thing he asks is sacrifice!*

Jesus spells it out in plain language, giving us steps 1, 2, and 3 without wiggle room for loopholes.

> Then Jesus told his disciples, "If anyone would come after me, let him deny himself and take up his cross

> and follow me. For whoever would save his life will
> lose it, but whoever loses his life for my sake will
> find it. For what will it profit a man if he gains the
> whole world and forfeits his soul?"
>
> —Matthew 16:24–26

Perhaps the disciples tucked this saying away, pushing it aside, assuring themselves that Jesus was speaking metaphorically. Remember, Jesus said this *before Calvary*. After Calvary there was no escaping the meaning of taking up your cross. The cross meant sacrifice. Giving up. Pain. Surrender to another's will.

In the medical world, we have three main avenues for the treatment of cancer: surgery, chemotherapy (the treatment of cancer with medicines), and radiation therapy. Looking at Jesus' one-two-three plan gives us insight into the life of love that God intends. It's the surgery, chemotherapy, and radiation our souls need to lift us out of the selfish cancer that squeezes the love out of the body of Christ.

1. Deny yourself

Deny yourself. This will never be a popular philosophy. In American culture, we easily understand the concept of denial of self *for the purposes of an eventual personal gain*. "No pain, no gain" is the mantra of our health and appearance enthusiasts. Professional athletes train hard, denying themselves the luxury of sleeping in and eating that second serving of potato chips during a favorite TV show. But I'm not so sure this is the type of denial that Christ was after.

I believe our call is to deny self for the *good of others*. Simply put, it's all about love.

What does 1 Corinthians 13 say? Love "does not insist on its own way" (v. 5a).

The ability to deny self in order to serve others is a consequence of heart transformation. Perhaps, as I am a surgeon, I should call it heart transplantation, except that may indicate that love would suddenly pump from our new hearts after conversion. I like the word *transformation* better as it implies an ongoing process. I believe it is a result of ongoing discipleship and attention to the health maintenance efforts we have already mentioned.

Love and service of others are inseparable. If you love others, you will be working for their good. The opposite is not necessarily so. We can do good works for a variety of wrong motives, and as we've seen, service without love at its heart is about as valuable as the clanging of a cracked cymbal. The love-service link is huge.

> Above all, keep loving one another earnestly, since love covers a multitude of sins. . . . As each has received a gift, use it to serve one another, as good stewards of God's varied grace.
>
> —1 Peter 4:8, 10

I believe the denial God is calling us to is intrinsically related to our calling to reach a dying world for Christ. Have any of you been tempted to think, *God is in control of everything. In his sovereignty he is going to save whomever he wants, so why should I suffer or deny myself?* Paul answers this common misconception.

> Therefore I endure everything for the sake of the elect, that they also may obtain the salvation that is in Christ Jesus with eternal glory.
>
> —2 Timothy 2:10

Just because God has elected his church is no excuse not to deny your own comfort for the sake of the gospel. Suffering and self-denial for the sake of seeing the lost come to Christ, *as long as love is the motivation,* is never wrong!

This is our calling, brothers and sisters, whether we like it or not. Christ suffered for us, to rescue us and win us unto himself, and we are to suffer as well, following his example to rescue the remaining cells of his bride.

> For to this you have been called, because Christ also
> suffered for you, leaving you an example, so that you
> might follow in his steps.
>
> —1 Peter 2:21

2. Take up your cross

I'd love to just skip this part. Nobody, certainly not me, wants to submit to the crucifying of his or her own flesh. But dance as we like, we can't sidestep the issue. Jesus proclaims it clearly enough. "Want to be a part of my band?" He points to a pile of crosses. "Take up a cross. It's the instrument I want you to play. Just follow my lead."

The cross always means paying a price. Always. And the currency is suffering.

The crucifixion that is ongoing is my daily death to sin. This means putting my desires behind those of Christ and others he has chosen to lead the church forward. That means sometimes others get to play lead fiddle, while I sit back and support the melody that God has chosen for them.

This issue of crucifixion will not be over until we see heaven and is to be an attitude that grows out of a transformed heart. As Paul says, it is a matter of necessity that we consider ourselves dead to sin.

> So you also must consider yourselves dead to sin and
> alive to God in Christ Jesus.
>
> —Romans 6:11

> He himself bore our sins in his body on the tree, that
> we might die to sin and live to righteousness.
>
> —1 Peter 2:24

> Those who belong to Christ Jesus have crucified the
> flesh with its passions and desires.
>
> —Galatians 5:24

When I deal with cancer from a surgical standpoint, I always follow certain principles. The cornerstone to success is the mandate that every bit of cancer be removed if the patient is to hope for a cure. That means I need negative margins. In other words, I cut out all that I can see to be cancer *and a margin of normal tissue.* If we cut through cancer at the margin, it is certain to haunt the patient again. If I misunderstand cancer's tendency to extend microscopic fingers into surrounding normal tissue, I'll cut away too little. This aggressive approach is justified because of the life-threatening nature of the disease. If it wasn't a big deal, I could cut close to the edge without concern.

Likewise, when dealing with my own cancer of selfishness, the Bible uses harsh terminology. "Crucify the flesh." I need to be certain that I am not doing the minimum I can get away with. I need to be sure that I have negative margins, that I have been appropriately aggressive with my treatment, *because this type of spiritual cancer is so deadly to the calling of the church: Love!*

> Put to death therefore what is earthly in you.
>
> —Colossians 3:5

Paul used language that everyone understood. We understand physical life and death. Certainly the Christians in Colosse understood that Paul was extending a metaphor comparing our need to address problems in our spiritual life in a similar way. A surgeon would say, "Aggressively cut away the cancer that is eating at you. Use negative margins! Don't stop until you are sure it cannot grow back." Meditatively read through this passage in Colossians, and notice that God doesn't call us only to a destruction of sin and its consequences. He calls us to restoration after the soul surgery is done. After the putting off, there is a putting on. Look at what he says a few verses later:

> And above all these put on *love*, which binds everything together in perfect harmony.
> —Colossians 3:14, *emphasis added*

A characteristic of cancer cells is that they have lost their normal adhesiveness, their ability to stay in association with the cells of their original location. Instead of being bound to others, they break away, starting new colonies elsewhere. A consequence of the transformation that God works in us as we apply ourselves to the discipline of spiritual health is the love that binds us to our fellow Christians.

3. And follow me

It has been said that imitation is the highest form of flattery. Look at any group of teenagers today, and you can see whom they idolize. Do they wear the shoes of the latest basketball stars? Do they speak the phrases of their Hollywood heroes?

Of course, it's not only the teens in our culture who are slaves of imitation. I also begin to think, talk, and act like those whom

I adore. The imitation of Christ is the essence of following him. Look at Paul's exhortation to the Ephesians:

> Therefore be imitators of God, as beloved children. And walk in love, as Christ loved us and gave himself up for us, a fragrant offering and sacrifice to God.
>
> —Ephesians 5:1–2

The two phrases "be imitators of God" and "walk in love" are joined by an "and," not a "but." They are one and the same. God is love. Walking in love is the every essence of imitating him.

When Jesus called his fishermen-disciples into relationship with him, the injunction was to

> "Follow me, and I will make you fishers of men."
>
> —Matthew 4:19

Again we see two statements joined by an "and." Following Christ is all about gathering others to him, and that happens naturally as a consequence of love, which is in turn the imitation of God. This isn't rocket science or brain surgery. The relationship is unmistakable: Following Christ means submitting to his way—sacrificial love for the world.

Lest you begin to think that this life of following Christ is all about suffering and self-denial (and it really is), let me make it equally clear that the life of love that Christ is beckoning us to is the fulfilling life of the fountain next to our selfish little play-puddles. Falling right on the tails of love in Paul's list of the fruit of the Spirit in Galatians 5:22 are "joy" and "peace." Yes, he calls us to a life of self-denial, but this is not a life bereft of pleasure. In fact, he has designed the greatest pleasure for us. Joy, peace, patience, kindness, and all the other fruit are harvested in plenty from the life-tree grounded in the love of God. In fact, as I've written before, I believe that living a life of love is the natural outgrowth of understanding just how passionate God is about us. And inherent in that love is the laying your life down for others that is at the heart of denying yourself and stands at the heart of the gospel.

> Greater love has no one than this, that someone lay down his life for his friends.
>
> —John 15:13

I am not asking you to deny yourself of every material pleasure. Hasn't our loving Father given the intelligence and creativity for mankind to produce many wonderful things that enhance and enrich our lives? But I am echoing Christ's call to deny ourselves of sinful passions that draw us away from his heartbeat.

There are many reasons why my patients neglect deadly cancer. Denial. *I've had this lump for so long. It doesn't seem to be hurting me.* Fear. *I remember another man from my village who had the same problem. He had to have surgery to remove his leg.* Ignorance. *I'm sure it will go away. If it's still here in a few months, maybe I'll seek help.* Poverty. *I could never pay the price required.*

Are there similar reasons I neglect to treat my selfishness? Denial. *I'm not so bad. At least I'm not like _____.* Fear. *I'm not going to ask my pastor for help. Then he'll never respect me.* Ignorance. *God doesn't really care about this.* Poverty of soul. *After I buy my sailboat, I'll help out the missionary family from my church.*

Don't be deceived. The warnings of falling in love with money are manifold. Paul warned Timothy that a desire for earthly riches leads down a road of "ruin and destruction."

> But those who desire to be rich fall into temptation, into a snare, into many senseless and harmful desires that plunge people into ruin and destruction.
> —1 Timothy 6:9

The cure for our cancer of selfishness is to actively cut away the offense.

> But as for you, O man of God, flee these things.
> —1 Timothy 6:11a

This is the essence of soul surgery. But God has additional chemotherapy, an infusion of fruit to take the place of spiritual cancer. He prescribes:

> Pursue righteousness, godliness, faith, love, steadfastness, gentleness. Fight the good fight of the faith. Take hold of the eternal life to which you were called and about which you made the good confession in the presence of many witnesses.
> —1 Timothy 6:11b–12

The language here is far from passive. "Pursue. . . . Fight. . . . Take hold."

In 1 Corinthians 14:1 we are told to "Pursue love." The Greek word translated "pursue" is used several other times in the New Testament and is sometimes translated "persecute." It is the root word used to describe Paul's activities (before his conversion, as Saul) in Acts 8, where it says a "great persecution against the church" arose (v. 1). Look at what kind of activity Paul used to "pursue" the Christians:

> But Saul was ravaging the church, and entering house after house, he dragged off men and women and committed them to prison.
>
> —Acts 8:3

Paul says we are to use the same energy in our quest for love!

Does this mean I am to go door to door, dragging men and women out of their homes and into a church building where they can be loved? Hardly. But from the use of the same word in 1 Corinthians, we can gain a better idea about how aggressive we are to be about pursuing a cure for our heart's self-centeredness.

Cancer. Deadly. Spreading, metastasizing unless there is appropriate treatment. Compromising body function, robbing the healthy tissue of nutrients and health.

Spiritual cancer. Selfishness. Loving only me. Taking and never sharing, resulting in "ruin and destruction" (1 Timothy 6:9).

I am writing as a fellow cell in the body of Christ. I face the same battles as you. In typing out these words, I feel God's gentle conviction. I am sure before anyone else reads this, I'll be led down the loving road of Matthew 16 over and over and over again. I need the surgery, chemotherapy, and radiation treatment of the Holy Spirit. I'll fall. But by God's grace he'll allow me to see the stone that tripped me.

So I'll deny myself, take up my cross, and follow my Savior down a suffering road into the joy and comfort of his love.

For Further Reflection

1. Is the "me, me, me" attitude of spiritual cancer ever at work in your life? With what results?

2. What did Jesus mean when he called us to deny ourselves? Why do you sometimes find this difficult?

3. What did Jesus mean when he called us to take up our cross? Why do you sometimes find this difficult?

4. What did Jesus mean when he called us to follow him? Why do you sometimes find this difficult?

5. Why do you sometimes ignore the spiritual cancer in your soul? What roles do denial, fear, and poverty of soul play in this? What can you do to allow God to overcome this cancer of soul?

Chapter Eleven

FINALLY LOVING ME

The most difficult person I've ever been required to love is me. I'm not unlovely, but I spent too many years not really believing it. I don't want to drag you through the total muck of my experience, but I thought an overview might assist some of you along the right path. And maybe you can avoid some of the pitfalls into which I fell facedown. For too long I treated God's beloved (me!) in a way I'd never treat another human being.

To help you understand, I'm going to have to uncover a few stones along the path I've taken. The biggest one to trip me up was something that spun me into heart-pounding condemnation and loomed large in my life throughout my teen years and on into my thirties. It didn't prevent me from pursuing a dream career in surgery and even success in the writing of multiple novels, but inside I was often miserable, always churning about something I'd done wrong. It was a beast that went nameless until I read a little book by a smart psychiatrist, Jeffrey Schwartz, M.D., *Brain Lock: Free Yourself from Obsessive-Compulsive Behavior*.

I'd heard of OCD (obsessive compulsive disorder) before and recognized some of the classic symptoms in myself along the way. Toward the end of college, I began struggling with compulsive behaviors such as excessive hand-washing and recognized at one level that my compulsions made little sense, but *I had to wash*. To do otherwise meant facing an avalanche of anxiety. Later I felt I'd beaten some of the symptoms, but it wasn't until I read Schwartz's book that I began to see how OCD hadn't gone away. It had only disguised itself and was now manifesting itself in a myriad of compulsive behaviors with a religious bent.

Some of you don't have the foggiest idea what I'm talking about. Others will read along and realize that they too have been battling this monster known as OCD. According to Schwartz:

> OCD is a lifelong disorder identified by two general groups of symptoms: obsessions and compulsions. Once thought of as a curious and rare disease, it, in fact, affects one person in forty in the general population, or more than five million Americans. A disorder that typically has its onset in adolescence or early adulthood, OCD is more common than asthma or diabetes.[1]

It's so common, but few seem to understand how OCD can get so tangled up in religious thought. Why bring this up here? Two reasons. First, it's likely that some of you will see yourself in these pages. All of us have obsessions and compulsions. It's the quantity of these that the OCD sufferer has that defines his or her condition as a real problem. And second, OCD binds many of its Christian victims in a tangle of obsessions about morality and guilt so tightly that they find it impossible to find peace and spend their years in quiet mental condemnation over real or imagined offenses. It is this second reason that compels me (here I'm using compulsion in a positive sense!) to speak out. I've seen little written about an area where statistically speaking, thousands of Christians are bound in needless torment. They sit quietly, poring over Bible verses about forgiveness and love, yet their obsessions of guilt and offenses prevent them from ever really believing the truth. Inside they churn, guilty and ashamed, not imagining that their sins are really atoned for, never able to fulfill the second greatest command to love their neighbor because it is contingent upon this modifier, "as yourself."

Schwartz defines obsessions as "intrusive, unwelcome, distressing thoughts and mental images."[2] "Compulsions are the behaviors that people with OCD perform in a vain attempt to exorcise the fears and anxieties caused by their obsessions."[3] Perhaps you've heard of someone with over-the-top anxieties about germs, sticky substances, body waste, or fluids. Others are familiar with hyper-concern over order, the possibility of harming others or objects (normal wear and tear on handled objects can cause off-the-chart concern for the OCD patient. *Did I mean to scratch that table?*), etc. Those are run-of-the-mill obsessions. Compulsions are the activities associated with trying to get rid of the obsessions: the washings, the double, triple, quadruple checking that the oven has been turned off or that the iron has been unplugged, etc. Hand-washing to get rid of germs, imaginary or real, is just one example.

For the Christian suffering from OCD, intrusive, unwanted thoughts can be devastating. Impure thoughts, pornographic images, fleeting curse words pass through all of our brains. But the OCD sufferer becomes overly concerned about them and in the process magnifies the intruder because of the attention. The Christian with OCD often becomes introspective about the source of these thoughts, and rather than recognizing them as junk thoughts common to mankind (and therefore unworthy of concern), their minds dwell on the thoughts, passing over and over the same mental ruts. They can become concerned about nonexistent spiritual attacks as the source and end up spending needless hours in the turmoil of self-condemnation. In short, where a normal believer can let an image or thought enter and exit, the Christian with OCD often cannot unglue a thought until a compulsion is obeyed. The problem is, the relief is short-lived. A minute later, there's something else nagging at the mind, begging to be examined and expelled.

In situations like this, laudable Christian behaviors such as confession of sin can become mired in compulsive behaviors accomplished to quiet the anxiety over the offensive thoughts. Sometimes the conscience of a Christian with OCD can be quieted only by a verbal confession to a close confidant. Don't misunderstand. Confession of our faults one to another can be helpful, but for the OCD sufferer, it can take an abnormal place and become an essential before the person can let himself or herself off the hook.

Harmful obsessions for the Christian with OCD can be a trip-up point for religious activity and confession as well, with the person needing to apologize for insignificant injury (which is not insignificant in the mind of the OCD sufferer).

People with OCD often carry a sense of excessive responsibility for comments made or actions done in passing, spinning in mental turmoil and compulsively needing to atone for imagined negative consequences by confession or retribution.

For too many Christians with OCD, healthy Christian disciplines are ruined, as they become just more ritual compulsions instead of life-giving sources of grace. From 1 Corinthians 13 we've come to understand that even good works, done without love, are as worthless as dust. Likewise, Christian activities, whether it be confession of sin or something else, when done as an OCD compulsion ritual, serve little good and in some cases can be very damaging.

How did I find freedom?

Just recognizing that the anxiety I was experiencing was part of a common disorder, just giving my problem a name, was a beginning down the healing road. Schwartz's four-step method is also an effective tool, one that I need to use over and over. I'll only mention them here and refer you to his book for further insight. Relabel, reattribute, refocus, and revalue are the memory jogs used to recognize a thought as a junk obsession and not something of value worth my reexamination. I must focus my thoughts elsewhere and move on.[4]

Not everyone who has difficulty forgiving himself or herself is struggling with OCD. But it's part of my story, and it does affect thousands of Christians who give mental assent to God's promise that because they are "in Christ Jesus," there is "no condemnation" (Romans 8:1), but inwardly the guilty feelings linger until they complete an OCD compulsion. Unfortunately, I believe OCD is like any other illness, a consequence of the fall of man, but because it affects the mind, it is often viewed differently by the household of faith.

These thoughts will just go away if I memorize more, pray more, confess more.

"Do you have negative intrusive thoughts? Don't you know you are to take 'every thought captive'? Take authority over these thoughts, and rebuke them in Jesus' name!" So the OCD

sufferer pays even more attention to the junk messages instead of just letting them slip away.

The essence of successful treatment is the recognition of the illness and a retraining or refocusing of the thoughts on the truth and away from the undesired obsession. For the Christian with OCD, this moment-by-moment vigilance is the core of taking "every thought captive" that Paul urges in 2 Corinthians 10:5. OCD sufferers tend to assign way too much importance to unwanted thoughts and end up consumed with self, mired in self-condemnation, and unable to lift his or her eyes to Christ for relief. I love the way Eugene Peterson's paraphrase (*The Message*) renders Romans 8:6.

> Obsession with self in these matters is a dead end; attention to God leads us out into the open, into a spacious, free life.

It's not just people with OCD who have trouble loving themselves. We all do. We're all made of the same stuff. For some reason, all of us struggle with this to some degree. There are several key reasons for our misery, and some of the same techniques that help the OCD patient refocus can help us all.

What are the key elements of this problem, which has reached epidemic proportions within the church today?

When I'm not loving myself, I'm not believing what God says about my identity. I'm looking only through my eyes, through human eyes, and not through the eyes of faith. God says I'm his child, that I'm redeemed, loved, forgiven, and free. At the point of our self-loathing, we're choosing to condemn what God has forgiven; we are in effect hating what he loves and punishing a person for whom God's Son has already taken the punishment.

Somehow it's easier to focus on our own guilt that we can feel than on God's truth that we have to accept by faith.

A second factor contributes to the problem of extending love toward ourselves. We've heard messages from ourselves that contradict the message of the Holy Spirit, the message that God loves us, that we are lovable, pure, and redeemed, a bride of inestimable worth.

This, I believe, is the essence. The heart of the problem is not that I need to learn to love myself, but that I learn to trust that God really means it when he says he loves me.

The teacher is greater than the monitor.

The apostle John speaks to us about the problem of self-condemnation.

> . . . for whenever our heart condemns us, God is
> greater than our heart, and he knows everything.
>
> —1 John 3:20

Pastor William Oden explains it this way. Remember back in elementary school when the teacher needed to step out of the classroom for a few minutes? The teacher assigned a monitor to take down the names of anyone misbehaving. Well, as soon as Miss Snodgrass was out of the room, you glanced over at Susie, the teacher's pet, sitting sweetly in the front row and busily doing her assignment. You remembered the time that Miss Snodgrass bragged to another teacher about Susie's model of the solar system. *Mine was better than hers. She didn't even have the correct number of moons around Jupiter, and mine did!*

Inside you churned. A moment later, your hand closed around the big pink pencil eraser that your mom bought you for art class. You extended your arm, wound up and let fly with your best pitch, scoring a strike right on the back of Susie's annoying little curls.

Susie screamed.

The monitor, a skinny kid who had had it in for you since you beat him in the fifty-yard dash, pointed a bony finger in your direction. "You're in for it now," he seethed. He wrote down your name on the chalkboard for all to see. "Miss Snodgrass will send you to the principal. You are so busted."

You started to sweat. *The principal! My parents are going to freak!*

The monitor shook his head and underlined your name. "You're bad."

The minutes passed in agony. The teacher was coming back. Judgment was promised. Your stomach was in knots.

Susie looked at you and stroked the back of her hair.

Miss Snodgrass wasn't back in class for even a second before the skinny kid started in. He pointed at you. "I saw it all. This despicable student threw an eraser and hit Susie in the head."

Susie rubbed her head and sniffed.

Miss Snodgrass looked at you. "Is this true? Did you throw an eraser at Susie?"

"Yes, ma'am." You lowered your head. "I'm sorry. I shouldn't have done it."

She walked toward your desk. You winced, suspecting she was going to eject you from the classroom. Instead she lifted your chin so that your eyes met. "You are sorry, aren't you?"

You felt your throat closing up. You were only able to nod your reply.

Miss Snodgrass smiled. "Then I forgive you." She walked to the blackboard and erased your name.

Forgiven! Off the hook! Yes!

An hour later, it was time for recess. And who did you meet below the monkey bars but your nemesis, the skinny kid the teacher named as the monitor while she was out of the room. He spat on the ground at your feet. "You are so busted. You're in trouble. What kind of person hurts a nice girl like Susie? You're disgusting! Miss Snodgrass has your number now."

You walked away, unconcerned, letting the words of accusation fall to the ground without penetration.

Why?

Because the teacher was greater than the monitor and had already forgiven you.

Sound familiar? Read 1 John 3:20 again. "God is greater than our heart, and he knows everything." When we find ourselves under guilty accusation from either our enemy or our own hearts, we need to be reminded that God loves us, has forgiven us, and knows everything. He is greater than our hearts, so we can let the accusations roll off our back.

When you find yourself feeling unworthy, groaning beneath a load of guilt, unload it to your Heavenly Father. The Holy Spirit gently reminds us when we have strayed. But he does not condemn. When the Spirit nudges you to repent, do it. But after you have laid a sin before the Father, leave it there and refuse to listen to accusations about your guilt. Perhaps there will be occasions when God will lead you to talk to someone you have wronged. But you must go with the knowledge that you are already forgiven by God. Going with a heavy weight of guilt on your heart will only hinder you from hearing the soft voice of the Spirit.

Remember, confession of sin is for restoration of fellowship with our Father. It is not necessary for our forgiveness. Christ's sacrifice paid for all our sin—past, present, and future—and our acknowledgment of sin before God is meant to realign our thinking with his. He has already forgiven us.

There is no reason for a Christian to walk around feeling guilty for past sins. Yet so many do. They wallow in the mud of their sinfulness, a self-flagellation of sorts. This behavior is a slap in the face of a gracious God. How dare we (in our pride) trudge through the snow of our guilt when he has already shoveled the driveway on our behalf?

It may be that you need to memorize a few verses to use as weapons in your battle against guilt.

> If God is for us, who can be against us? He who did not spare his own Son but gave him up for us all, how will he not also with him graciously give us all things? Who shall bring any charge against God's elect? It is God who justifies. Who is to condemn? Christ Jesus is the one who died—more than that, who was raised—who is at the right hand of God, who indeed is interceding for us.
>
> —Romans 8:31b–34

> There is therefore now no condemnation for those who are in Christ Jesus.
>
> —Romans 8:1

> But the Lord GOD helps me; therefore I have not been disgraced; therefore I have set my face like a flint, and I know that I shall not be put to shame. He who vindicates me is near. Who will contend with me? Let us stand up together. Who is my adversary? Let him come near to me. Behold, the Lord GOD helps me; who will declare me guilty?
>
> —Isaiah 50:7–9a

We are at war. Make no error here. Don't be lulled to sleep because it is not occurring in a visible realm. When accusations fly, fight back! We can nestle ourselves against the heartbeat of God. He is our help. We stand in his presence on the authority of the blood spilled on our behalf. Nothing can separate us from him, certainly not the accusations of man, the devil, or our own hearts.

False Propaganda

Recognition of the war should help us realize that our enemy is spreading false propaganda about us. He not only does this to our face but also before the throne of God. In Revelation 12:10 he is revealed as the "accuser of our brothers" who "accuses them day and night before our God."

He whispers the same lies over and over. It would seem that we would soon recognize his voice as the poison it is. What are his favorite lines?

One is, "You're the only one struggling with this problem." The truth is, we're all made of the same stuff. A belief that no one else is fighting the battle that you are will make you feel isolated and alone, exactly where Satan wants you. The Bible directly counters this false propaganda.

> No temptation has overtaken you that is not common to man.
>
> —1 Corinthians 10:13a

Here's another devilish favorite: "It's always going to be this way. You're never going to beat this problem." If you find yourself believing this, you'll soon be dining with despair. Unleash the sword of the Spirit to counter this.

> And I am sure of this, that he who began a good work in you will bring it to completion at the day of Jesus Christ.
>
> —Philippians 1:6

The third lie follows on the tails of the first two: "If you act this way, you must not be a Christian at all." This is craziness. Your sin only proves one thing—you need a Savior! If correct behavior was the ticket to heaven, there would be no need for grace. Yes, we're sinners, but that only qualifies us as grace recipients.

> . . . for all have sinned and fall short of the glory of God, and are justified by his grace as a gift, through the redemption that is in Christ Jesus, whom God put forward as a propitiation by his blood, to be received by faith. This was to show God's righteousness, because in his divine forbearance he had passed over former sins.
>
> —Romans 3:23–25

For some of us, the lies about our unworthiness came through parents, relatives, or teachers. "You'll never amount to anything." "You're stupid." "Don't bother me now. I don't have time for you." If you have suffered in this way, you need to begin to bathe yourself in the truth from the Bible about your identity in Christ. This will take time, but with prayer and focused study on the reality of being a beloved child of God, righteous, forgiven, an heir with Christ, and the focus of God's love, I believe the Holy Spirit will begin to replace the old hurts with his whispers of love.

In order to love ourselves, we need to recognize the lies of our enemy and reject them as the poison they are. Then we need to refocus on the truth of our identity as his beloved.

Practically, how can you love yourself? Don't neglect your spiritual or physical health. Spend time with the Father. The realization that God is the ultimate source of joy and satisfaction means that allowing ourselves to treasure him above all things is the very best way to love ourselves because in treasuring him, we find true happiness.

It may seem an ironic twist. The best way to love ourselves is to fall in love with God. When our passion for him is foremost, our focus is naturally shifted away from our unworthiness and onto his worthiness. Away from our sin and onto his grace. Off of our work for him and onto what he is doing with or without us. The by-product of loving Christ is always joyful, peaceful, and loving fruit. Spiritual wellness springs up in my soul when I am passionately dwelling in the shower of his love.

Love yourself by loving him, trusting that he really means it when he says, "I love you."

For Further Reflection

1. What are some ways that Christians suffer the malady of spiritual OCD? How does this show itself, if at all, in your life?

2. Why aren't spiritual disciplines such as Bible reading, prayer, and confession of sin enough to cure spiritual OCD?

3. In what ways do you believe your own ideas about who you are rather than what God says about who you are? With what consequences?

4. How does the illustration of "the teacher is greater than the monitor" help you have better balance in this area? What key Scripture speaks directly about this?

5. To which lie from our enemy ("You're the only one struggling with this problem"; "You're never going to beat this problem"; "If you act this way, you must not be a Christian at all") do you most easily fall victim? What can you do to keep from believing these pieces of false propaganda?

Chapter Twelve

THE ULTIMATE TEST: LOVING OUR ENEMIES

It was a warm September morning in 2001 that changed our world forever. For many, the concept of safety evaporated into the illusion that it's always been.

That day for me has been seared into my memory with a permanence that is possible only with an up-close-and-personal encounter.

On September 10, 2001 I was sitting in Yankee Stadium waiting for the New York Yankees to take the field after a rain delay and listening to my family's adventures of their day touring the city. As I ate overpriced hot dogs, I heard about how Joel, my oldest son, purchased a souvenir picture taken from the top of the Twin Towers that afternoon. It was one of those gimmick photos that swapped Joel's face for King Kong's as he gripped the side of the World Trade Center. In his hand he held a defenseless woman, complete with my wife's head, tilted toward his open mouth.

Joel groaned and looked up at the sky, which remained dark and foreboding, offering little hope for a letup in the downpour. It had been a long day, but this was going to be the highlight, a baseball game in Yankee Stadium. After ninety minutes of wet skies, we watched as Joe Torre walked across the field shaking his head. A minute later, the cancellation was proclaimed over the PA system.

I tried to comfort my son. "Don't worry, Joel. This game might be rained out, but tomorrow rain won't matter. They never cancel Broadway." We had September 11 tickets to our first Broadway production, a celebration of percussion and dance known as *Blast*. Little did I know.

I was attending a General Surgery Board Review conference, being held in a hotel in Secaucus, New Jersey. From our window we had an excellent view of the New York City skyline, a view destined for change during our visit. During my meetings, my wife and son spent time seeing the big-city sights. When making out the schedule, they chose September 10 to go to the World Trade Center and September 11 to stay in the hotel to do homework assignments.

On the morning of 9/11, I was sitting in a darkened lecture hall taking notes. I began to hear some murmurings from the back of the room. I got up to stretch my legs and soon heard the rumors of an attack. I rushed to my room to find my son staring out the window at the Twin Towers, both belching large clouds of black smoke.

Joel had just seen the explosion from the second aircraft as it penetrated its target. With wide eyes, he brought me up to speed, and we watched as the Twin Towers crumbled to the ground.

Within an hour I was on a school bus, with police escort, taking us to set up a first-aid triage station to assist in caring for victims. Hour by hour we waited, listening to the rumors, watching the smoke rise, and gazing skyward as American fighter jets crisscrossed overhead. The information came to us in the form of urgent, inaccurate updates. *Twenty thousand potential victims. Possible biological hazard loaded on one of the planes.*

I separated myself from the hubbub of activity where we'd set up dozens of cots and where IV fluid lines were primed and ready. As I paced, looking toward the sky, I remember longing for the security of something familiar. Suddenly all I wanted was to be back home in Virginia, throwing a baseball with my boys.

This was my first encounter with the mysterious world of Muslim extremism. I'd never really thought much about the fact that Christians were thought of as enemies by anyone, except in my understanding of God versus Satan. But as of 9/11, a new understanding grew for me and others about the way America was viewed from within the Muslim world. To many, America was Christian. And that, apparently, was sufficient reason to hate us.

Love God. Okay, I get that. Love your neighbor. Uh oh, now the trouble begins. Love your enemy. *Come on, Jesus, that may sound good in Sunday school, but this is real life!*

If you've been tempted by that thought, join the club. You can have your turn chairing the committee after I'm through.

Let's look at this radical concept. Jesus wanted his followers to be defined by one thing—love. And not just the run-of-the-mill, love-the-lovely-people-who-love-you love. There is no mistaking this concept. No shoving it off under some theological carpet. He had to have meant something else, right?

Wrong.

> "You have heard that it was said, 'You shall love
> your neighbor and hate your enemy.' But I say to
> you, Love your enemies and pray for those who per-
> secute you, so that you may be sons of your Father
> who is in heaven."
>
> —Matthew 5:43–45

Jesus means exactly what he says. We are to love our enemies. To whom, exactly, is Jesus referring? I believe Jesus didn't need to explain in detail, because the disciples understood perfectly what he meant.

Dietrich Bonhoeffer, German pastor and theologian, nonviolently resisted Hitler's politics, was imprisoned, and was killed by S.S. Black Guards in 1945. What he spoke about loving our enemies carries the weight of his personal sacrifice. He explains just what Jesus meant by our "enemies."

> In the New Testament our enemies are those who
> harbour hostility against us, not those against whom
> we cherish hostility, for Jesus refuses to reckon with
> such a possibility. The Christian must treat his enemy
> as a brother, and requite his hostility with love. His
> behaviour must be determined not by the way others
> treat him, but by the treatment he himself receives
> from Jesus; it has only one source, and that is the
> will of Jesus.[1]

Ouch. We are unable to define our enemies by the way we feel about them. As we are not to cherish feelings of hatred, the definition of *enemy* changes focus from those we don't like to those who don't like us. An enemy isn't someone we hate. An enemy hates us.

And an enemy isn't someone who doesn't like us because of our quirks or our misbehaviors; an enemy is one who unjustly harbors hostility against us.

Perhaps I should clarify. I am talking about personal enemies, not a nation's enemies.

So just what does love for our enemies look like?

> "You have heard that it was said, 'An eye for an eye and a tooth for a tooth.' But I say to you, Do not resist the one who is evil. But if anyone slaps you on the right cheek, turn to him the other also. And if anyone would sue you and take your tunic, let him have your cloak as well. And if anyone forces you to go one mile, go with him two miles."
>
> —Matthew 5:38–41

Showing favor to someone undeserving is grace. Loving an enemy is an example of second-mile grace, showing love above and beyond what we deem as reasonable.

Thankfully, God isn't into "reasonable" love. If he were, he wouldn't have sent his Son to die for our sins, and we would have no hope of anything but condemnation, forever.

Sometimes loving God, loving my neighbor, and loving myself seems like second-mile grace, doesn't it? None of that comes easy. But perhaps that has something to do with our lost focus, where programs and more programs are exalted above my personal heart transformation.

Let's look further at the second-mile concept of loving our enemies. Luke's Gospel expounds a little further:

> "But love your enemies, and do good, and lend, expecting nothing in return. . . ."
>
> —Luke 6:35a

Paul fleshes this out even more, making it impossible to misunderstand what this kind of grace looks like:

> To the contrary, "if your enemy is hungry, feed him;
> if he is thirsty, give him something to drink; for by
> so doing you will heap burning coals on his head."
> Do not be overcome by evil, but overcome evil with
> good.
>
> —Romans 12:20–21

These verses tell us exactly what loving our enemies looks like. Blessing, praying, not resisting, going beyond expectations, feeding, giving a glass of cool water.

But how?

Remember what we learned when we were talking about loving our neighbors? The same principle applies here. It's the Nike principle: "Just do it." When we obey and reach out to assist our enemies, we might find the enjoyment of the act following, like a caboose being pulled along behind the steam engine of obedience and the coal car of faith. "Just do it" is the beginning. We need to obey and pray that God would change our hearts so that we actually come to experience the emotion joining the core action. Remember, he desires that we really love our enemies, not just act in a love-like way.

Making Loving an Enemy Easier

A few considerations can help us make loving our enemies an easier task. First, remember that *you and your enemy are both made of the same stuff.* We're both flawed. Both need redemption. At the cross, the ground is level. Again quoting the incomparable Bonhoeffer:

The love for our enemies takes us along the way of the cross and into fellowship with the Crucified. The more we are driven along this road, the more certain is the victory of love over the enemy's hatred. For then it is not the disciple's own love, but the love of Jesus Christ alone, who for the sake of his enemies went to the cross and prayed for them as he hung there. In the face of the cross the disciples realized that they too were his enemies, and that he had overcome them by his love. It is this that opens the disciple's eyes, and enables him to see his enemy as a brother. He knows that he owes his very life to One, who though he was his enemy, treated him as a brother and accepted him, who made him his neighbour, and drew him into fellowship with himself. The disciple can now perceive that even his enemy is the object of God's love and that he stands like himself beneath the cross of Christ.[2]

When I realize, as Bonhoeffer has suggested, that I was an enemy of Christ, that I cradled hostility toward Christ, then those who hold hostility in their hearts toward me are seen in a new light: soldiers in the same trench. So this is the first key to loving an enemy: realizing my own wretchedness. When I am acutely aware of my own sin, I'm less likely to stand in judgment of my brother. It is this judgment that stands as a hurdle to loving.

The second consideration is that *we need to see our enemies through the eyes of God.* His are the eyes of grace. He loves without condition. In order to love the unlovely, I have to be a channel, not the source. Obedience in this area follows a willful decision to believe the truth that whomever God has created is a subject of his love and should be of ours also.

A third consideration deals with *an understanding of spiritual warfare*. As Christians, we do have a true adversary, but our enemies are not the non-Christians. "Remember, non-Christians are not the enemy. They're victims of the enemy."[3] This valuable reminder keeps us focusing our fight where it ought to be: prayer. If I understand that non-Christians are enslaved by my enemy, I need to rely on God's work to set them free. My job is to *love them*, not convert them. Conversion is a heart matter and is initiated only by the Holy Spirit. The joy is seeing love open the way. This is the essence of evangelism. I'll talk a bit more about that later. For now, let's look at an example of this kind of love in action.

Corrie ten Boom and her sister Betsie suffered in a Nazi concentration camp after having been turned into the Gestapo by Jan Vogel. Corrie faced the temptation to hate head-on. From her own pen we read:

> What puzzled me all this time was Betsie. She had suffered everything I had and yet she seemed to carry no burden of rage. "Betsie!" I hissed one dark night when I knew that my restless tossing must be keeping her awake. Three of us now shared this single cot as the crowded camp received new arrivals. "Betsie, don't you feel anything about Jan Vogel? Doesn't it bother you?"
>
> "Oh yes, Corrie! Terribly! I've felt for him ever since I knew—and pray for him whenever his name comes to mind. How dreadfully he must be suffering!"
>
> For a long time I lay silent in the huge shadowy barracks restless with the sighs, snores, and stirrings of hundreds of women. Once again I had the feelings

that this sister with whom I had spent all my life belonged to another order of beings.

Wasn't she telling me in her gentle way that I was as guilty as Jan Vogel? Didn't he and I stand together before an all-seeing God convicted of the same sin of murder? For I had murdered him with my heart and with my tongue.

"Lord Jesus," I whispered into the lumpy ticking of the bed, "I forgive Jan Vogel as I pray that You will forgive me. I have done him great damage. Bless him now, and his family. . . ."[4]

Corrie's attitude perfectly illustrates our three points. She discovered the ability to love an enemy when she saw Vogel through the eyes of a Father who sent his Son to die in Vogel's place. She realized she stood on equal ground with Vogel in front of the cross. Vogel was no longer her enemy. He was *a victim of her enemy.*

When I am tempted toward hostility instead of love, I must find my way down the Calvary road. I must die to myself and remember the level ground of love beneath the suffering Christ. He loved me when I was his enemy. He chose me when I was in sin. This humble recognition will allow me to lay down my precious hostility and leave it in the shadow of the cross.

God shows his love for us in that while we were still sinners, Christ died for us. . . . For if while we were enemies we were reconciled to God by the death of his Son, much more, now that we are reconciled, shall we be saved by his life.
—Romans 5:8, 10

How can I hate those whom God loves?

Too often my justification reveals my own desire to be on the throne. My feelings were hurt. I was devalued in some way. I was offended because one of my rights was violated by another. When I am tempted in this way, I need to quickly recognize the false gospel of pride that is preventing me from loving my enemy. Only with the cross in constant focus can I begin to care more about forgiveness than justice, more about love than getting even.

How dare I despise and judge another when my own unredeemed heart is full of malice, murder, lust, idolatry, and every other vice?

Can I not see that the person on whom I have catapulted my hostility is a slave to the same master that I faithfully served until my salvation by grace alone?

Within Africa, I have found my outreach ministry focus among a tribe that serves Allah as God and Muhammad as his prophet, a group so isolated from Christ that only one in ten thousand names the name of Jesus as God and Lord. This tribe, as a whole, misunderstands Christians and their faith, believing only what they have memorized in their Islamic schools, hardly a place for accurate information about the gospel or its followers. From within their home country, Islamic extremists have flourished, launching their attacks on Christian "infidels" in the name of Allah.

As a Christian, I am viewed by those extremists as an enemy. To me, this thought is absurd. If anything, our outreach to assist these people is the only true love they've ever experienced.

I certainly do not consider Muslims my enemies. I agree with Brother Andrew, founder of Open Doors, who says, "We must start spelling 'Islam' as, '**I Sincerely Love All Muslims.**'"[5] Antagonists to the gospel are sometimes converted with reason, sometimes converted by a stimulating truth presentation, but never converted without love.

It does not seem unusual to me that this door has opened for me after my close encounter with Islamic terrorism on 9/11. If anything, that's *exactly* how God usually does things.

It's all part of his call to participate in second-mile grace.

For Further Reflection

1. Love God; love your neighbor; love your enemy—which of these do you find most difficult? Why?

2. How would you define *enemy*? Who are your enemies (be honest)? In what ways does God want you to show them his love?

3. Do you agree that you and your enemies are made of the same stuff, that the ground is level at the foot of the cross? Why or why not?

4. Do you find it easy or hard to see your enemies through God's eyes? Why? What can you do to experience this more clearly or more consistently?

5. Are you most like Betsie ten Boom or Corrie ten Boom? Are you willing to pray Corrie's prayer, making it *your* prayer? Do so now.

Epilogue

THE LANGUAGE OF THE GREAT COMMISSION: HANDS OF CHRIST, FEET OF CLAY

I feel like it's the fourth quarter, with two minutes left and time for a hurry-up offense. It's time to put the ball in the end zone, but everyone's bone-weary and in need of an inspiration infusion to get the job done one more time. The coach has one time-out left to sketch out a winning plan.

God has gathered his team on the sidelines for final advice. He pulls out the clipboard and draws a red circle around one word.

Love.

That's it? What about fancy ministry tactics? Three-step salvation messages? Effective witness strategy?

The Coach smiles and points to the one word on the page. "Just love," he whispers.

When God chose one word to define his character in 1 John, he used love.

When Jesus urged his followers to love, he used the strongest language possible: not advice, not a suggestion, not even a proposition, but a command.

When asked what can be done to inherit eternal life, Jesus' answer can be summed up in a single word. Love.

Of faith, hope, and love, all essentials in the Christian backpack, Paul said the greatest of all was love.

It's the first in the list of fruit of the Spirit in Galatians 5:22.

When Paul spoke of the qualities we needed to pursue in Colossians 3, he said:

> And above all these put on love, which binds everything together in perfect harmony.
>
> —v. 14

Love stands at the heart of the gospel, the core of God's motivation and plan to rescue his bride. Now, just to be perfectly clear on this, I am not talking about a wimpy, overly soft love that says, "I love you no matter what you do" in the sense that whatever we say or do is okay. Rather, this love, God's love for us, says, "Your wrong thoughts, words, and actions are despicable in my sight. I cannot wink at or overlook any of it. Nevertheless I love you. I want to pardon you and make you brand-new, and that's why I sent my only Son to pay the price of your sins and win your forgiveness in him." Yes, love stands at the heart of the gospel—love that was demonstrated at the cross where the totally innocent Son of God, our Lord Jesus Christ, died so we could live. In that sense the cross stands at the heart of the gospel, because it was there that God's love shone most clearly and most powerfully. And once we come to know God through Jesus Christ, that love is to flow out from us to all who are around us. Jesus couldn't be clearer. Love was to be the way that everyone who wasn't a Christian would look on and understand. *Oh, they're Christians. I can see it in their behavior.*

Paul says that without love, we're dead in the water. Ministry fails. Evangelism falls flat. Our witness is void. *Come on, my good deeds must be worth something! Surely God notices.*

Not if they're devoid of love. Then every effort is useless. That's why Paul says we are to pursue love. I like the way it reads in *The Living Bible*, a helpful paraphrase:

> Let love be your greatest aim!
> —1 Corinthians 14:1a

My mother is a character. In order to understand what I mean, you have to read that sentence with a bit of a southern Virginia accent. In Virginia, being a character is mostly a good thing. Of course, it often carries the slight connotation of being a bit cantankerous or mischievous. She has brilliant white hair and a dimpled smile and blue eyes that look right into your soul.

I remember one day when I was about thirteen years old. Mildred (that's my mom's name) came rushing into my room, eyes wide. "Harry Lee," she called, her voice sharpened with urgency.

Something was wrong. The right side of her normally symmetrical smile had drooped. On one side, her upper lip lay flaccid as she talked, dragging along behind her facial expressions that animated the rest of her face.

"Thomething's happened to me," she said. "I can't whithle." She attempted to close her lips around a small circle, but the right side of her mouth refused to cooperate.

She stood over me, pathetic, demonstrating over and over the lost skill. The wind blew through her lips, escaping without adequate restraint to sound a clear note. "Phhheee, phheee."

She shook her head. "I thhhink I'vef had a thstroke."

I stared at my mother. Her face was etched with concern. Her eyes were searching my face. She wanted me to help.

Having grown up in a medical family, I'd heard of a stroke before. Strokes were bad. Mysterious, paralyzing illnesses. My grandfather had plenty of them and was too crazy in the end, a real character.

I didn't know what to say. I remember sitting on the edge of my bed, the double one I'd inherited from my parents. I touched the surface of the red velour bedspread that Mom had bought for me. "Mom . . ." I said.

She stared at me, helpless, afraid, mouth drooping. This was it. She was going to start drooling like Grandpa before he died. I just knew it.

Then she smiled, and I could tell by the twinkle in her eyes that she'd just yanked my chain. Big time. "Nahh," she said. "I justh got back from the dentisth, and my mouth ith still numb," she slurred.

"Mom!"

Life with Mildred in the driver's seat was rarely dull.

What does all this have to do with love? A lot, really. You see, the dentist had injected my mom's mouth with a local anesthetic. These medicines are a miracle for surgeons. What happens is that the nerves that are designed to carry messages back and forth to the brain are temporarily deadened. Microscopic channels on the surfaces of the nerve are blocked, and in effect the message of pain cannot be transmitted up the nerve to the brain. So the pain stimulus is still there, but the brain doesn't get the message. Likewise, the nerves carrying messages back to the muscles are also blocked, so the muscles can't respond to the command.

In my mother's case, her brain was saying, "Whistle," but the right side of her mouth didn't get the message because the nerve carrying the message refused to cooperate.

In the case of the body of Christ, the message he is sending is love. But some of us behave as if we've had a dose of lidocaine or some other local anesthetic because we're not transmitting the impulse that begins with God and is intended to touch a suffering world. Are we so busy with kingdom activity that we've blocked the impulse of love that Christ is constantly transmitting?

It's time some of us began to understand a basic concept. God is invisible. We see him through the eyes of faith. The impulse of his heart toward the world is love. This love prompted the greatest gift of all.

> For God so loved the world, that he gave his only
> Son, that whoever believes in him should not perish
> but have eternal life.
>
> —John 3:16

When Jesus walked the earth, he was the supreme manifestation of God's love for us. Now, since Jesus is no longer present in bodily form, guess who gets to be the manifestation of God's love?

Us.

That's right.

It's time for a key concept.

The central reason for the body of Christ metaphor used in the Bible is so we will begin to see ourselves as the avenue for the impulses of God.

His heartbeat becomes ours. His impulses originate with Jesus, our head. But his impulses initiate action *in us*.

He is love. He is incapable of less. His love finds expression through his body. That's us! We are the fingers of Christ to touch the world. For so many, we are the way they will know the heartbeat of God.

We have been brought together into the functional unit known as the body of Christ for one reason:

> . . . we are to grow up in every way into him who is the head, into Christ, from whom the whole body, joined and held together by every joint with which it is equipped, when each part is working properly, makes the body grow so that it builds itself up in *love*.
>
> —Ephesians 4:15b–16, *emphasis mine*

As his body, we are intended to function with the unity of purpose seen in the magnificent setup of the human body. An impulse originates in the mind of God, then is simultaneously transmitted to thousands of cells awaiting the command. In an intricate plan that coordinates the appropriate inhibitory and excitatory centers, the message is interpreted and obeyed. Muscles respond, each cell in unity with its neighbor, each cell supplied with all it needs to obey the command under direction of the head. By grand design, every provision for prompt obedience has been readied.

As we function as the hands of Christ touching the lost, the sick, and the hungry, our actions will naturally point to Christ as the source. The head, not the hands, gets the glory. By design. And that's glorious. And the world worships in response.

> "You are the salt of the earth, but if salt has lost its taste, how shall its saltiness be restored? It is no

longer good for anything except to be thrown out
and trampled under people's feet. You are the light
of the world. A city set on a hill cannot be hidden.
Nor do people light a lamp and put it under a basket,
but on a stand, and it gives light to all in the house.
In the same way, let your light shine before others,
so that they may see your good works and give glory
to your Father who is in heaven."

—Matthew 5:13–16

What I'm saying is nothing short of the most liberating news of all. We have been connected to an unending source of power, love, and redemption. As channels, our responsibility begins and ends with readying ourselves to transmit the impulses of God's heart to the world. The end of all Christian disciplines is this: more of Christ and less of me. The more I can be a pure love channel, the more effective I'll be in executing his mission, not mine.

But we have this treasure in jars of clay, to show
that the surpassing power belongs to God and not
to us.

—2 Corinthians 4:7

We are the hands of Christ. That could be a heady message. But we're to remember that we are earthen vessels, mere "jars of clay" who define our worth because of the presence that we carry, a presence who chooses to define himself with one word: love. We are the hands of Christ. But remember, we have feet of clay. Humbly we serve, not seeking our own glory, but his.

We live in a day of unparalleled progress. Technology, genetic engineering, scientific discovery, and communication present ever-greater chances for good. But we also live in an age of unparalleled violence, poverty, and oppression. Slavery, child prostitution, pornography, and the problem of child soldiers sit at the world's table beside organized crime, government corruption, terrorism, and the threat of nuclear disaster.

The problem with the world lies within every human heart. Unredeemed, man is filled with the seduction of money, sex, and power.

Where is hope to be found?

The answer is the body of Christ. We are the sole agents of true love that changes the world one heart at a time.

> . . . the riches of the glory of this mystery, which is
> Christ in you, the hope of glory.
> —Colossians 1:27b

Here is the truth of this glorious mystery. Christ indwells us by his Spirit. And thus within the clay wrapping of human flesh is the hope for the world today—Christ in us!

Ask most Christian scholars about the mission of the church today, and I suspect you'll hear talk of finishing the task of the Great Commission, the growth of Islam, and the problem of a multitude of unreached people groups. These are, indeed, items of priority and deserving of concentrated effort.

But in a day when the church is wrapped up in programs, seeker-sensitive worship services, and contextualized missions, love remains a nebulous concept, something so "out there" in quality that we've failed to curl our fingers around it to bring it into our own experience. So we tend to ignore the spiritual transformation necessary in our own hearts (in essence, an exchange of my old heart for a heart that flows with love) and concentrate on the things we can do—that is, programs, programs, programs. Beware! Programs, even when efficiently executed, abundantly funded, and expertly staffed, are nothing without love. Remember the "clanging cymbal" of 1 Corinthians 13.

This book is not a call to abandon our programs or our mission to make disciples of every nation. I'm only a voice asking us to think again about a concept so basic that we seem to rush past it in our efforts to do the work of God. Love is an "of course!" But for many, it's such an "of course" that it's ignored, to their own peril.

Hopefully you've seen within these pages a small glimpse into what this love looks like. This love, this benevolence, will look differently depending on God's specific design for different members of his body. In many cases it will be ordinary acts of kindness. In others it will look like the extraordinary acts of grace described in the Sermon on the Mount.

> "And if anyone would sue you and take your tunic, let him have your cloak as well. And if anyone forces you to go one mile, go with him two miles. Give to the one who begs from you, and do not refuse the one who would borrow from you."
>
> —Matthew 5:40–42

In these few verses Jesus sets the bar extremely high. Should we despair? Of course not. If we were anything but channels of the impulses of God's heart, we wouldn't even show up for the game. But God has made it clear that he wants to touch the unlovely with his love. And we are his avenues of choice.

Called to Love

I've met many missionaries who speak in certain, if not spiritual-sounding, terms about God calling them to specific ministries around the world. I don't doubt them. But I think we've overspiritualized the concept of a missionary "call," so that many of us wonder if we can take part in evangelistic ministry. *Am I called?*

This book has been all about simplifying the call of Christ to his body. In one simple word, it's all about love. Maintain the basics of spiritual health , and we will fulfill the call of God by design, by becoming the channel of love straight from the heart of God. Then we can love whomever God puts in our path. That's our calling. Simple but life-changing.

When Kris and I were considering leaving my surgical practice in North America to serve in a hospital in Kenya, we wrestled with this concept. The opportunity for service in this way was open in front of us. *But are we called to do this?*

I'd heard crazy stories about well-meaning Christians confirming their special callings by circumstances, some of which bordered on the bizarre. At the time I was considering a call to Kenya, I developed a rash on my left forearm, a rash that looked similar to a map of the African continent. But was that a call? No. It was poison ivy.

Our "calling" came in the form of obedience to a verse impressed upon me from the book of Galatians.

> So then, as we have opportunity, let us do good to everyone. . . .
>
> —6:10a

I could see that service in Kijabe was good. I saw that the opportunity to serve was open. Beyond that, we asked God to close the door if we were not to serve in that way. The opportunities to stop us were many. How would we finance such a journey? Who would care for our house? Would my practice be able to find a replacement? Who would care for my little schnauzer? In each situation or concern, God was faithful to keep the opportunity open in front of us, even down to providing for Calvin, our little dog.

God's calling to love remains in front of every member of his body. We must love as we have opportunity. Our calling doesn't have to be more complicated or spiritual than that.

This book hasn't been about turning our backs on the Great Commission. It's about the realization that the way to fulfill our calling is by being intentional about understanding Jesus' command to love God and to love our neighbors as ourselves. Success in any missionary endeavor depends upon it.

Let me repeat myself. I am not urging us to put less emphasis on fulfillment of the Great Commission. Our message to the world is the gospel: Christ came into our world to save undeserving sinners. The language to communicate that message is *love*.

The language to communicate the Great Commission to the world is *love*.

Communication in a cross-cultural, cross-language context can be a minefield. One afternoon shortly after my arrival in Kenya, I was leaving the outpatient clinic area. I wanted to say in Kiswahili, "I'll see you later." The exact translated phrase in Kiswahili is, "We will see each other later" or "*Tutaonana.*" Unfortunately, what came out of my mouth was close but not close enough.

I looked at the nurses who'd been assisting me. "*Tutanona,*" I said, waving.

The Kenyan nurses laughed, covering their mouths with their hands.

"What?" I asked, dismayed. "What did I say?"

A nurse smiled. "You said, 'We'll all get fat together.'"

I laughed along with them over my mistake. One dropped letter, and the word changed meaning completely. Fortunately, I hadn't said, *Tutaoana,* which means, "We'll get married."

That could have been a costly mistake indeed.

Also, when English is spoken as a second or third language, the subtle nuances are lost, and the result can be comical. A patient looked at me with all seriousness as he said, "My mother has pain when she sleeps upside down." The mental image of my patient's mother hanging possum-like from the ceiling made me smile. But I understood what was meant. She hurt when she positioned herself on her stomach. But what was said was comical.

A few years ago, Gary Chapman wrote a best-seller entitled *The Five Love Languages*. In essence, he pointed out that love has different ways of expression and that individuals respond better to love expressed in a particular way. Some primarily respond more positively to gifts, some to touch, some to words, and so on.

What I'm saying is this: finding a way to communicate the gospel is paramount. The most effective way to communicate that message is love. Someone once said, "Build a bridge of love that is strong enough to carry the weight of the message you need to give." For us, the bridge is love. The composition of the bridge will be different depending on the giver and modified to suit the receiver.

The health-care profession in America is under a barrage of pressures related to business principles, high costs, reimbursement issues, and looming malpractice lawsuits for bad outcomes that have nothing to do with poor medical care. But the truth remains that compassionate medical care remains a powerful way to show love. That's why mission hospital outreaches continue to be effective spearheads for communication of the gospel. Medical care transcends language and cultural barriers and offers a quick opening into the most intimate aspects of human life. Illness creates crisis, and in crisis people begin to ask the important questions about eternity.

I use medicine as an example because it's the life I know best. But other service-oriented professions are equally effective as instruments for love's communication.

Love means concentrating more on changing me, and less on changing you.

What I'm suggesting isn't easy. Loving yourself can be tough. Loving a neighbor, tougher still. Loving an enemy may pose the highest hurdle. But God hasn't asked us to participate in the impossible. He intends for his church to love by design.

In order to fulfill our calling to love, we need to be disciplined about spiritual fitness. We cannot expect to be successful in our programs if we haven't been disciplined about infusing health into our anemic, immune incompetent, cancer-ridden souls. By priority, we must put more emphasis on personal heart transformation and less on programs to change others. More on basics, less on tactics. More on love and compassion, and less on getting the words out in a polished manner. *In essence, more on changing me, and less on changing you.* When I love you independent of your worth, maybe you'll change too.

In the end, the rewards are rich. I've never known such joy as when I've merely obeyed and let God love someone through me.

Are you up to the challenge? Will you begin to focus on the main thing and the ingredients that will insure a successful effort? Remember our theme: God has imprinted us with his love. It is to define his body, but the message will be scrambled if we ignore the basics. I need daily biblical nutrition. I need a continual hydration with the love of God. I need a constant saturation with the gospel of grace. I need regular times of rest and refreshing.

Loving. Being loved. It's a cycle that will occur as naturally as respiration within the context of the healthy body of Christ.

Love. The heartbeat of God. The next time you're tempted to think that love is a concept so fluffy and ethereal that it can't be realized in your own experience, think again. Love is the most basic and fundamental component of the Christian life, intended as the very defining feature of our faith.

How do we start?

To borrow a phrase from Nike once more, *Just do it!*

For Further Reflection

1. Why is love so primary in the gospel and in the Scriptures? Is love—God's love flowing through you—that important to you?

2. Do you agree that "some of us behave as if we've had a dose of lidocaine or some other local anesthetic because we're not transmitting the impulse [love] that begins with God and is intended to touch a suffering world"? Why is this so? What can we do about it?

3. Do you really see yourself as a "jar of clay"? So how can you hope to make an impact on others, on the world?

4. "We are the sole agents of true love that changes the world one heart at a time." Do you believe this, or is this just a noble but impractical Christian cliché?

5. What has God called you to do or be? What part does love play in all this? What can you do day by day to fulfill that calling? Will you start (or continue) today?

NOTES

Chapter 2: The Love-Shaped Void

1. Beat Jost, *The Final Chapter of World Missions: Releasing the Hosts of the Eleventh Hour* (Pasadena, CA: William Carey Library), pp. 2–3.

2. John Piper, "The Goal of God's Love May Not Be What You Think It Is"; http://www.desiringgod.org/ResourceLibrary/Articles/ByDate/2000/1515_The_Goal_of_Gods_Love_May_Not_Be_What_You_Think_It_Is/.

Chapter 3: A Controlling Passion

1. John Piper, *Let the Nations Be Glad* (Grand Rapids, MI: Baker, 1993), p. 13.

2. Harry Kraus, *Breathing Grace* (Wheaton, IL: Crossway Books, 2007), p. 22.

Chapter 4: Loving Your Neighbor with the Purple Pants

1. Arthur C. Guyton and John E. Hall, *Textbook of Medical Physiology*, eleventh edition (Toronto: Elsevier Saunders, 2005), p. 51.

2. Dallas Willard, *Renovation of the Heart: Putting on the Character of Christ* (Colorado Springs: NavPress, 2002), pp. 130–131.
3. Ibid., p. 130.

Chapter 6: Spiritual Insomnia

1. Arthur C. Guyton and John E. Hall, *Textbook of Medical Physiology*, eleventh edition (Toronto: Elsevier Saunders, 2005), p. 740.

Chapter 7: "Can I Have a Drink of Water?"

1. Arthur C. Guyton and John E. Hall, *Textbook of Medical Physiology*, eleventh edition (Toronto: Elsevier Saunders, 2005), p. 361.
2. Ibid.
3. Ibid.
4. Ibid.

Chapter 8: Breathing Grace

1. Harry Kraus, *Breathing Grace* (Wheaton, IL: Crossway Books, 2007), p. 15.

Chapter 9: Failure to Thrive

1. Randy Alcorn, *The Treasure Principle* (Sisters, OR: Multnomah, 2001), p. 75.

Chapter 10: The C-word

1. Dallas Willard, *Renovation of the Heart: Putting on the Character of Christ* (Colorado Springs: NavPress, 2002), pp. 130–131.

Chapter 11: Finally Loving Me

1. Jeffrey M. Schwartz, *Brain Lock: Free Yourself from Obsessive-Compulsive Behavior* (New York: ReganBooks, 1997), p. xiv.
2. Ibid.
3. Ibid., p. xvi.
4. Ibid. The four-step method is the core of this wonderful little book, and I'd recommend it for anyone personally suffering from

OCD or for family members who need to understand just how the OCD mind works.

Chapter 12: The Ultimate Test: Loving Our Enemies

1. Dietrich Bonhoeffer, *The Cost of Discipleship* (London: SCM Press Ltd., 1959), p. 132.

2. Ibid., pp. 134–135.

3. Walter L. Larimore, M.D. and William C. Peel, ThM, *The Saline Solution: Participant's Guide* (Bristol, TN: Paul Tournier Institute, Christian Medical and Dental Society, 2000).

4. Corrie ten Boom, *The Hiding Place* (New York: Bantam Books, 1971), p. 180.

5. "Muslim World—The Greatest Challenge Facing the Western Church Today," June 24, 2005, Open Doors press release; http://www.opendoorsuk.org.uk/press/articles/archives/001023.php.

SCRIPTURE INDEX